# BECOMING UNRULY

## CONVERSATIONS ON CHANGE FROM THE CLASSROOM TO THE BOARDROOM

## DR. LA ROYCE BATCHELOR

FriesenPress

Suite 300 - 990 Fort St
Victoria, BC, V8V 3K2
Canada

www.friesenpress.com

**ISBN**
978-1-5255-7774-1 (Hardcover)
978-1-5255-7775-8(Paperback)
978-1-5255-7776-5 (eBook)

*1. SELF-HELP, COMMUNICATION & SOCIAL SKILLS*

Distributed to the trade by The Ingram Book Company

*If you want to think differently, innovate regularly, navigate change and be change; read on. This book offers a way to examine the status quo and alter it dramatically!*

Dear Reader:

My long wait is over! I've been pushing for La Royce to write this book for a long time, mainly because of how the teachings within this book flipped my perception of things, people, and many other aspects of my life. Nearly 7 years ago, I took a class I had heard was, well... "different" from the standard college courses. I had been struggling internally on whether I wanted to stay within my major of commercial aviation which I truly loved and was quite good at but felt something was off. I took La Royce's class as a trial run to clear my brain a bit and expand my scope of learning, hoooo boy was I in for a ride.

The materials, explanations, scenarios, and deep-thinking exercises within this aptly named book, *Becoming Unruly*, give you the tools to take a different look into, onto, and outside of your world. I truly believe this book will allow you to change quite a few aspects of your life, or at the very least how you think about the "world" you exist in. I don't say this from just reading the book, but from experiencing this book first-hand as a student, a mentee, a business owner, a scholar, teacher, and a simple person existing in this crazy and fun world. I should state this isn't necessarily a "transformative" book, where you will suddenly and magically transform your life for the better after reading this book. I will bet though, that it will feel like that as this book will have you do a few particular things we as individuals rarely do in our society. *Becoming Unruly* puts into light all the processes, reasons, purposes, promises, and underlying reasons we do things in our lives. How do we value these? Why do we value these? Do we need them? Many more deeper dives topics lay waiting for you to discover and delve into yourself, so I won't give any hints or promises.

From what I personally have experienced from the learning from La Royce and this book's content, is that the materials in these pages WILL stay with you. I'm not just some random person stating this after using them one time 7 years ago, I practice these, learning many times a year, and I'm not alone. I've pushed so hard for this book because of how the materials in this book saved me nearly 7 years from the deep lull of frustration and self-depreciation I kept putting onto myself. I have gone from the student example within this book's content that was struggling in their own head, to someone who has advocated for the learnings in this book in many aspects of my and other's lives.

My last part for you to consider picking up and reading this book is the level of detail and explanation on how to implement these not into just your life, but into a classroom. As an Instructional Designer who has read many books about changing classrooms and teaching pedagogies, many don't lay out the goals and aspects with good details let alone instructions, and expectations. This book breaks that mold to highlight and lay out all the details you need to incorporate these methodologies and pedagogies into your learning environment. I don't just recommend you read this book, but I DARE you to; this book will push you. It'll make you consider many parts of your life and teaching seriously, but for the betterment of both. I've been eagerly waiting for La Royce, one of my best friends and mentors, to make this book's teachings available for the masses so they can have the potential to change themselves like I was able to.

Be Unruly, and never stop being so.

-Jonathan Puhl, M.S. Instructional Designer

Dear Reader:

Dr. La Royce Batchelor is one of the wisest and most charismatic women I have had the blessing of being in my life. Being a black-belt karate instructor, a bad-ass wife and mother, and undenying dog-lover, she is a jack of all trades. She has shown through her triumphs and trials that life is never easy, but if one rides through the waves, peace will come.

Although I did not take any classes with La Royce, I did have the pleasure of being a fly on the wall in some of her classes, observing her students complete different adventures and experiments. I was amazed with these creative situations La Royce presented to her students in class, and I was just as in awe when I read this book myself. Upon reading sections like The Challenge and PB&J, I was reminded of memories of being in that classroom, and it made me curious to want to try some of these strategies on my own.

I envison La Royce as the wise mentor who is posing questions about the constructs of our daily lives and how some of these are false ideals. She aims to question what we all place value in and want to change the way that our lives are structured; *Becoming Unruly* does just that. It will place you in situations you may have never given any thought to, or make you look at something that seemed so simple before but now holds so many different avenues of thought. Of course, a reader can certainly pursue the content cover to cover, but this book also provides the unique opportunity to focus on certain aspects of education, business, or even life by jumping from one section to another for when you really need it most.

Throughout reading this book, I found myself questioning the way I do things, what I note as valuable in my character, and what I want to change, no matter the internal struggle that may occur. I also found myself thinking of ways to incorporate some of these activities, like the Pick-Up Game or the Adventure begins, into my middle school curriculum. Wouldn't it be interesting to see how much loose change students could find around them and use it as a reward for strengthening their skills of observation? With the ever-constant routines that the majority of my students do daily- School, Extracurricular Activities, Sleep- how many of my students would be willing to try something new in their life to see the benefit of changing up routines? How willing would _you_ be?

Overall, this book has helped me see that in order to become unruly, some messes may occur, and in the life of a middle school English teacher, messes happen on a daily basis! I recommend you take up this book if you are looking for a major change to your life, or even if you are comfortable with your life but don't know that a change in perspective may be helpful to you, I suggest you put some time into reading this book. While this book does require an introspective look into the way you structure your life and world around you, sometimes when given the chance, those inner thoughts are the ones that speak the loudest towards making your life be what you want it, not what it has become to be.

-Kat Puhl, middle school English teacher

# Preface

As I finished writing this book and got it off to the publisher for last checks, the world changed because of Co-Vid. Quarantines were enacted. Social distancing became the norm. The world slowed enough to hear the birds and watch the smog clear. The price of gas plummeted. Lucky people worked from home. Students attended classes online. Gyms and community clubs were closed. Online communities for exercise and business ventures exploded. Kids continued their education online while at home. Universities closed their doors continuing education online. Bars and eateries were closed except or delivery, drive thru, or pick up orders. Millions of people lost their jobs. A stark reality hit the world. Living paycheck to paycheck and in debt doesn't work. The rules of the game as many had come to understand it was clearly not to their benefit, but to their detriment. Many people fell into a malaise. Many saw it as an opportunity to do things they'd always wanted to (within the Co-Vid guidelines of course). Still many more were left with questions; questions about their relationships, work, money, goals, life, and what WAS normal.

I have to admit, Co-Vid did little to change our lives. Our sons took online classes. My husband already worked from home one day a week. I was working on another book. We were not impacted financially as we have always lived frugally.

But for my publisher, things got busy. People who had been meaning to finish a book finally did and many more started the process. This book was finished and about to roll into production. In the Great Pause that occurred, I took a moment to think about this book, this process, and this experience. The publisher asked me if I should narrow the target market in light of the changes in the world. She asked if I'd like to focus on women. My immediate reaction was NO. This book is based on nearly 30 years of teaching in both higher education and corporate settings. The participants were from every background, age group, gender scale identity, and from more countries than I can remember. This book isn't about separating people into target markets. It's about a tool for change. I will say it's more for people under 35 than over. Participants over 35 had a very difficult time with some of activities that challenged their lifelong thinking and habits.

I'm hoping the world doesn't return to the way it was. The business as usual model simply wasn't working. I'm hoping you've picked up this book looking for a new way. This book doesn't offer a path, but it does offer a way to examine our choices and how we might change them. If you were questioning things during the Great Pause (Co-Vid) but without structure and without resolution, then this book will help a lot. This book will offer clarity where the media and governments only offer platitudes and news bites.

# An Introduction

I sat on the edge of tears. It had been a motivational, but emotional day. There had been many speakers, but three specifically seemed to understand exactly where I sat. After 28 years in higher education, a PhD, four countries, five universities, more than 6,000 students, I sat unemployed and unmotivated. But every path had been leading me here. Everything I had ever done or created had been leading me, no pushing me, to write this book. My family and friends had been telling me for a decade that I needed to write this book. My students urged me, over and over again, to write this book. Colleagues would insist that I needed to write this book. And still, I hesitated. At this point, it was more than stubbornness or a lack of time. So why?

Negative self-talk. The voice in my head, the box I had constructed for myself, kept telling me that no one will read this book. Millions of books exist. After decades in higher education I knew that books took years to publish and were usually out of date when they hit the market. I knew that books were old technology. After all, it took a major Herculean effort to get my students to read a book I recommended. Only some of them would actually read it. I believed that some books could be a catalyst for change but thought that there are so many other more famous authors out there so my book would go unnoticed.

Superfluous.

Unnecessary.

This book would be a waste of time. You're a researcher and a public speaker, you know nothing about writing a book. You're a teacher and a coach, not an author. But on that day, it seemed so clear that writing this book was what I was supposed to do. I would be continually lead, back to this place, until I wrote this book.

I do believe that there are some things that we need to do and somewhere inside us, our subatomic particles demand that we do certain things. My entire body was sure that I needed to write this book. I walked home from that event crying and shaking. It was a very long four kilometers in the early evening of a beautiful June. I have no doubt that I was the source of conversation for many other pedestrians that day. "There was this lady, walking, talking, crying; all by herself!" Getting past one's own negative talk can be quite difficult. The struggle continued for days as I tried to figure out how to write this book.

I borrowed my son's laptop and started to make an outline. I started with the goal of 1200 words each day. This exercise, over time grew into the book you have in your hands now.

# Acknowledgements and Gratitude

I must thank my family, my loving and encouraging sons and my stalwart and supportive husband. I must thank several friends such as Natasha without whom I would not have even begun. I must thank every person who read an early draft; their feedback was essential. My small posse of former students who became family were and are essential for my wellbeing. I must thank every student who emailed or messaged me, not knowing I was writing this book and telling me just how important these activities had been for them. Finally, I must thank all my students because I do all I do for them.

# So, let's begin

All journeys begin with a single step and all journeys change us and create stories. Whatever it is you hope to achieve; it begins with a single step. How does every story begin? It begins with a decision and a little background.

I hope you enjoy this book. I hope it challenges you. I hope you get angry, cry, shake, question, and in the end, learn something about yourself and others. More importantly, I hope you become unruly.

Becoming unruly means becoming someone who pushes their boundaries and examines what is or has been. All rules and limitations should be questioned. If one thinks "I can't" that's a clue that there is a rule somewhere that dictates that response and that limitation must be examined. The unruly do not believe that things have to be the way they are; they understand that things can change. Unruly believe they can change themselves and they can impact how things change. The unruly seek out opportunities to change and grow. The unruly question constantly and enjoy unraveling the puzzles. Don't feel like you're unruly? Keep reading, you may be more unruly than you think. Besides, there's always a chance to push aside the rules to reveal more meaningful elements.

Similarly, it may become clear that you have been fighting change. Change can be very painful and difficult. I'm afraid there's no easing this process. You may find you revisit change, embrace it, only to find you've slipped back into old habits that must again be broken.

## How to use this book

This book is intended to draw attention to the beliefs and habits that may be holding you back or confining you in a box. Perhaps you also see people you know in the boxes included in this book. We all live in boxes, containers, boundaries of our own making. Perhaps it is someone else's box that limits your relationship. Most do not realize the extent to which they confine themselves and their thinking. A rare few begin to see that their own limited thinking is their major obstacle to their goals. But how do we change that thinking? How do we create new habits of thoughts? As in all science, nothing can change without intense and mindful observation and examination.

In leadership, we often struggle with tools to assist others in their journey, after all, it is best to open the door and let the student step through. When working in groups, we often see tensions and varied paths and approaches, but often lack the ability to articulate why one path is better than another. Simple activities, such as those in this book, have been tried and tested in the corporate environment as well as in higher education classrooms, for all leaders to examine different modes of operation and thinking and to choose the philosophies and behaviors they believe will serve best. Offering an exercise or two to groups or teams will reveal much about the thought processes behind ingrained habits and perhaps areas of tension.

This book contains the experiential learning activities developed, tested, and proven over decades of teaching in higher education. Experiential learning has become a buzz word in education. But like many things that become popular, the meaning and functional elements become diluted. Some practices are indeed experiential and each experiential learning element is different with varied depths and uses. Some professionals have been using case studies exclusively and believing they are engaging in quality experiential learning. Others believe that experiential learning must contain volunteerism. But I believe that experiential learning is varied and vast. The key is to engage people in an experience either mentally, emotionally, or physically. Creating experiential learning objects is actually quite simple and I will also include hints along the way for educators to create their own.

This book is not just for people trying to improve their situation, nor is it just for educators or leaders. It is for anyone looking for tools for analysis and situational change. If you're looking to create change, read on. If you are having difficulty navigating change, read on. Teams may use these activities to uncover speed bumps or barriers to effective collaboration. Individuals may use these activities to explore ingrained almost unconscious barriers that may result in self sabotage. Educators may use these activities to explore a variety of concepts and to instill vigorous questioning in student habits.

## Act First

In most books, there are concepts that are discussed then some activities and maybe some journaling. This book flips that paradigm and begins with an activity then explores the concepts behind what that activity reveals. Journaling is great for insight, but not for change. For real change we need to get out of our comfort zone and do things.

The debrief includes information for the classroom, individuals, corporate settings and ideas for leadership. Each section concludes with a review and summary questions to ensure maximum efficacy. In 28 years of teaching, in every class I begin with an activity. This has proven to be disquieting for many students hoping to just sit in a room and take notes then take an examination. Engaging with the material is the most effective way to retain information and to alter perspective.

In most situations, students ask first about the rubric for the activity. They want to know how they will be graded so they might alter their responses to achieve the highest grade possible. But this doesn't work in life. It only works in school. School is temporary and not an accurate reflection of life. Educators say they are educating students for success in life, but actually, rarely do. There are no multiple-choice tests in life. There are no essays with a clear rubric to follow and no one is assigning grades as a result. I hear you. There's that one argumentative person shouting that they do educate for life success and life does have a rubric. Respectfully, no, it doesn't. It's quite simple. You're either happy or you're not. I refuse to give a rubric for these activities and simply restate the activity. Why? Because it doesn't matter what I want or what I can grade. What matters is what you invest . and what you get out of the activity.

I urge you to do the activities first. Take your time. Don't over think them, just do them honestly and with the full expectation that the activity is designed to show you something you may not see. Reflect honestly, perhaps begin a journal. Don't try to game the activity, don't try to win or give the answer you think I expect. After all, I'll never see them. Don't try to fulfill some preconceived notion of who you are, that is indeed a box; a limiting concept of who you are and what you can do.

I have put off writing this book for a decade because I know only too well that self-development books only help if the reader does the work. Unlike a lot of books, this book does not seek to give you a recipe; that would be creating another box. But this book seeks to illuminate the box and provide options as to how to carve a way out of those limitations. The content of this book is meaningless unless the reader also does the activities. Think of it as a game and invite others to play with you. That often makes many of the activities and challenges in the book a lot more fun. Choose people with whom you'd enjoy a deeper and richer relationship and, of course, those you trust. I get it, I hear you saying, but I don't want anyone to know what I'm reading or doing; they'll judge me. I'm just doing some reading. And we just revealed limitation or box #1. Again, students taking my classes have had no choice and realized that they could have deeper richer relationships if they were just authentic or genuine with people rather than to hide thoughts or experiences. Companies paid me, and the participants knew this, to conduct activities. They often would try to do as little as possible because they were being paid to be there. And box #2 is revealed. What could possibly be so embarrassing that you'd not want to include others in the exploration? Besides, doing embarrassing things together often removes the sting. We have become a society of superficial relationships presenting a Facebook, Instagram, snapchat, twitter, or whatever social media acceptably filtered face. In the end, we remain alone and separated out of fear that someone may actually get to know us.

I can't emphasize this enough that in my nearly 30 years of teaching, my students had no choice but to do the activities. Those activities, invariably, were the tools needed for more than

6,000 university students in four countries to find a path to success. These activities have been tested again and again. Each term students would review the course and remark on how the activities were the key to unlocking learning and insight that changed their lives. My students have done amazing things with these tools from starting businesses, to pursuing higher degrees, to campaigning and being elected to office, to climbing the corporate ladder. All paths begin by understanding where you are.

Perhaps you are a teacher seeking new ideas about how to reach students or illustrate certain beliefs and behaviors. I was where you are now. I could see the students bored with education. They had learned through their high school or other educational experiences that school was just something you had to get through rather than something that engaged you. As an educator I also thought that if I just cared enough students would engage with the content. But I soon realized it's the magical combination of meaningful experiences and caring professionals that engage people. Please use all the activities and even alter them for your area or discipline. This is where change begins.

## You are here.

But where is here? Here is a place where most of us find ourselves. We seek a change. We seek inspiration. We seek to understand events or behaviors. We seek to improve relationships. This is a place of questions. All change begins with questions. Often so many answers become apparent that we cannot grasp them all. Take what you can. Go slowly. Return to the activities when you need to. Treat this as a workbook. There are no wrong answers.

As students enter my classroom for the first time, they know immediately that my classes will be different. I often play music.

I teach barefoot. I greet each person as they enter. I arrive early. There are usually treats. Students realize that their standard approach to class may not work in this situation and begin to open to the experiences ahead. As class begins, I converse with students, not lecture. I walk around the room. In this way students are eased into opening up to the activities. By looking for this book and reading the overview, it becomes clear that this book is different. You too have pushed aside expectations and become increasingly open to what lies ahead. If you are a former student and buying this book to recapture that classroom experience; thank you. But realize that while these are the activities you may remember it was the sharing of the experience that made them more acute.

This book is also iterative. What do I mean by that? As we destroy limiting beliefs that confine us, sometimes we build new ones. Then we outgrow those boxes and we need to find a way out again. Personally, I know that I live in a 7-9 year cycle. Every 7-9 years, I require dramatic change and challenge. Every 7-9 years, I must destroy the old box I've built, free myself, and begin again constructing new behaviors with new understanding and new tools. You, like me, may have read many books or listened to audio books or pod casts, attempting to break free. But over and over again, I come back to these activities. They work each and every time. Each and every time I learn something new. These are by no means all the activities I use when I teach. These are the activities that have been reported to have the greatest impact and the ones that can be delivered in this format; a book.

Well begun is half done is often said. If you begin well, your journey is half done and the work will be that much easier. So, begin with an open mind and a willingness to participate. I can hear the doubt in your mind from here! "Oh, I'll just read it, I'm sure the activity elements can be a thought exercise and I won't have to actually DO them." If this is what you believe, return the book. You're not ready to see what the activities will reveal. In conferences, or at speaker events, people are always hesitant to do the activities for fear of looking foolish. If fear is holding you back, you've already learned something. You've learned that what others think is more important that your own growth, your own happiness.

To begin, chart where HERE is. What are the joys of life? What are the challenges or frustrations of life? What is the goal? Perhaps there is more than one. Who is there to support you? Take some time and write down these responses. This is here.

## Here for me

Here for me is unemployed and I HATE being unemployed. I must be working. (But more on that later.) After years of education and hard work, after disaster and moving and three countries, I am unemployed. I still feel so full of ideas. I still feel like I can change the world; but how? Without students, without a university, how do I change the world? How do I help people?

How do I do what I do without the BOX of a classroom or a university?

I'll clean the oven. That will help. I'll bake and make amazing meals; that will help. I'll walk the dogs and teach karate. I'll ask others what I should do. Write a book they say. Start your own thing they say. See, I understand all too well.

Every time I've started a venture I had some idea of how to begin; where to begin and why. This time? I have no clue. Write a book on what??!!

I'm in midlife with a PhD which most corporate entities find useless and most higher education institutions find necessary. But I have insufficient published works for a university and too many for the corporate world. I am unorthodox which both corporations and universities despise, in spite of what they profess.

I have a mortgage and two kids in college. The entire weight of our financial requirements lands on my sweet husband. So unfair. I failed. After all, he said he married me for my earning potential. Ok, so perhaps that was a joke, but I'm definitely not pulling my own weight. Right now, I'm earning nothing.

But I am nothing if not resilient. I must bounce back. I must do the unexpected because that's what I do best. I am unruly.

BOUNCE

# PART ONE

---

## The Box You Didn't Know
## You Were In

# CHAPTER 1

# The Rules

*Activity #1:*

Please write a detailed response to this question.

What were the rules when you were a child?

## Merriam Webster Definition of rule

*1 a : a prescribed guide for conduct or action*
*b : the laws or regulations prescribed by the founder of a religious*
*order for observance by its members*
*c : an accepted procedure, custom, or habit*
*d (1) : a usually written order or direction made by a court regulat-*
*ing court practice or the action of parties*
*(2) : a legal precept or doctrine*
*e : a regulation or bylaw governing procedure or controlling conduct*

## Unpacking Meaning

How we define the things in our world is important. What we call them or name them is very important. Understanding language and learning that it creates our reality is life changing. We must realize that it is usually a difference of language and understanding that is at the core of conflict and impasse. We disagree because we see words and concepts differently.

The first step is to define terms. It's important to understand there are two types of definitions. There are connotative and denotative definitions. Denotative definitions are those that come from a dictionary or other vetted source. They are often widely accepted. They contain no controversy. These are the vocabulary words we learn as students. These are the expert agreed constructs that provide discipline specific lenses. It's also important to note that even experts may not agree on a definition. Many scholarly articles begin by defining terms. A quick survey of almost any topic in the scholarly journals reveals that no one agrees on definitions.

Connotative definitions are those that we add to language out of experience. Each person's experience is different creating a slightly different definition. We stack on experiences on top of definitions to illustrate the term. Each person's connotative definition is unique. This will be important when we start to pull apart definitions of rules.

Most students begin by understanding rules through experience. They begin with the connotative meaning. They start by thinking about what they thought were the rules when they were children. A lot of my students wrote answers like a curfew, sharing, chores, homework, grades, cleanliness, mealtime, or respectful attitude and language. They did not begin by defining the word: rules.

This in and of itself is telling. Without questioning and exploring a definition, we can't be sure we are discussing the same idea. Most students begin exploring this question with examples from their own experience. That is the connotative meaning. However, to see the unique limitations we've created, we must begin by examining the denotative meaning and then discovering what's been added or extra.

We have to ask how we came to define the term that way.

What situations or people played a role in our personal definition of the term?

How did we first understand restrictions placed on us?

What would be the consequences of violating those restrictions?

What was the purpose of those limitations?

## Some Examples

Bedtime is a common practice. Parents set a time that they believe provides the best sleep for children. Children require a lot of sleep for brain development. Establishing a routine for children stabilizes the changes and provides a structure upon which children can build trust. We create safe havens for their bedrooms. We buy and read books to stimulate intellectual growth. What if we violated bedtime?

Based on this foundation, we, as adults, set an expectation of a bedtime. We create routines around preparing for bed, washing faces, brushing teeth, reading stories. The routine for bed is something that is carried forward into adulthood. Children who were read to, often become adults who read before bed. Of course, there were those times in high school or college when we explored all-nighters and staying up late. People proclaim they are night owls or early risers as if it a product of DNA rather than learned behavior. As children, we often had nap time. But as adults somehow this is no longer acceptable. Naps are seen as weakness or a lack of productivity. Naps will interfere with a solid sleep at night. Sleep patterns are often one of the first rules students consider.

Consider a curfew. Many people had to be home at a certain time. Parents would set a time that everyone had to be home. Perhaps it was 10 pm or when the streetlights came on or when the town siren went off (a Midwest small town thing). Outlining this from multiple perspectives, it makes sense on many levels. First, it could be a safety issue. Depending on the age of the individual, it may simply be unsafe to be out of the house after a certain time. From a health perspective, ensuring plenty of rest requires an individual to be home in bed and sleeping for a prescribed period of time. Peace of mind is always difficult for parents and families. When family members are out it can be emotionally taxing as worry overtakes reason.

In many families we learn to share our belongings, our food, our time, or common entertainment elements such as the television. Again, from a parent's perspective, sharing builds many necessary skills such as respect for someone else's belongings. Sharing a meal builds relationships and as we share that meal, we also share time. How do we share our time in order to build a relationship? What do we share of ourselves to build trust, compassion, understanding, and affection? We learn to share resources such as a vehicle in order to create opportunities for transportation, but also to be mindful of expense and responsibility. We often share books or entertainment and in that shared entertainment, we also share joy or sorrow.

Many young people have to do chores. As a child, each Saturday morning, my sisters and I spent that time doing chores. Nothing else could happen until all the chores were done. We had to clean our rooms then proceed to do other chores that were age appropriate such as laundry for the week, mop floors, mow lawn, wash the car, or clean the bathrooms. The sooner we were up and had our chores done, the sooner we could enjoy the Saturday. Many of my students also share that they had to do chores. Avoiding chores had consequences such as a loss of freedom or the removal of certain privileges. Chores teach many valuable lessons such as personal property maintenance and responsibility as well as self-reliance.

The requirement of doing homework or earning certain grades may be to instill a certain level of work ethic or to ensure proficiency for success in a career. Completing homework may ensure a concept is practiced in many different environments. Report cards and grades create an opportunity to discuss constructive criticism and opportunities for growth. The emphasis on diligence toward schoolwork and striving for good grades is a way for families to create pathways for success that historically may not have been accessible due to a class or caste systems.

Many families create rules around personal hygiene or respectful relationships. Preliminarily, these may not seem connected, but in fact they are. Maintaining one's health and hygiene are indeed respectful; not only to oneself, but to others. The care and maintenance of health can become quite complex. Simple habits such as oral hygiene can avoid many health issues. Learning to care for oneself can also create an empathy for others. Large families learn quickly that shorter time in the bathroom often means everyone gets some time. Similarly, speaking in respectful tones and using appropriate language often means that their point will be heard and respected. Yelling only serves to increase the overall volume and distance the perspectives, vilifying those in conversation and making meaningful conversation impossible. From this we learn the difference between and inside voice and an outside voice.

The list of rules may be unique to your experience. Someone from another family, from another unique limiting construct may have very different operating procedures.

My mother once arranged for me to stay with a friend of hers over a holiday break from college. My regular accommodations were closed for that holiday but working over the holiday would be quite profitable. After only two days and nights, my mother's friend greeted me at the door after a shift at work. She told me this arrangement would not work out. I worked too late. I showered too early. My work (a server at a local pool hall) was not appropriate work for a young woman. Clearly, she and I had very different ideas of rules for life.

Writing down the rules and why they were in place may help us to understand their function at the time. My mother's friend was an elderly woman, twice my mother's age that had a very different understanding of the limitations or rules placed on women. But it is also clear that rules must change. For example, the curfew set by my parents when I was 10 is likely no longer necessary nor helpful. If I had not made arrangements with my parents, I had to be home for dinner, which was 5 pm. As an adult, I often finish work at 5 pm, making it impossible for me to also be home at that time. It is clear that at some point we learn to create our own rules.

# What rules are you still adhering to even though they no longer serve you?

When we examine the definition of "rules", it is clear that the rules are created by someone to guide behavior or action. However, there is a distinction. As children we are incapable of understanding the difference between a rule and an expectation. A child perceives both rules and expectations as the same thing. These are the constructs required in the household. Children also perceive the displeasure of others acutely. Often this displeasure also creates unspoken rules and expectations. The difference is that rules are often discussed, rationalized, and justified. Whereas expectations are created more subtly and sometimes are not as clear. Rules are more easily dismantled and new ones created as we mature. However, expectations shift without warning and are often carried throughout life without examination, rationalization, or justification. Similarly, there is family culture. Again, children often conflate rules, expectations, and family culture into a mix of something they perceive all as rules.

# Now, let's look at expectations.

*ex·pec·ta·tion*
*plural noun:* ***expectations***
*a strong belief that something will happen or be the case in*
*the future.*
*"reality had not lived up to expectations"*
*a belief that someone will or should achieve something.*
*"students had high expectations for their future"*

Understand that I am a rhetorician; I examine language. I spend time examining the meaning of words and the meanings they accumulate. I examine how words are used and the impact they have on people and situations. Most people do not. I am driven to unpack what is the denotative and connotative meaning of words and phrases. Conversely, many believe that language is common and therefore everyone must understand it. But understand that meaning is constructed mentally and often in isolation. We may read a definition, but the word takes on a functional meaning as well. We rarely spend time discussing in detail the meanings of words as we believe other people carry the same dictionary definition and cultural definition. However, consider there is also an interpersonal definition. Through our own experiences, we may begin to see certain words differently.

Not long ago there were discussions over the definition of marriage. There were religious, legal, cultural, and compassion-ate definitions. The definitions were used both inclusively and exclusively and created destructive discord. This was a difference in denotative and connotative meanings of the word marriage. There were even some differences in what could be considered denotative meanings as some people utilized religious based texts and others legal based texts. Even agreeing on the refer-ence material used for a definition can create conflict.

Consider for example the word love. Is it a noun or a verb? The dictionary meaning talks about an emotion, a strong emotion. And yet, we as a culture throw the word around quite casually in some situations and profess it quite cautiously in others. Love can carry, with it, other emotions such as fear or joy or remorse. It can dictate actions, rules, and expectations. We often demonstrate this strong emotion, but how? There are so many ways in which we show love and each and every word we learned, not from a dictionary but from the people in our lives. A single word can mean such vastly different things to people, that it causes conflict because they do not understand the other person's definition or understanding of the word.

What about a phrase like "Take care of dinner." What does that mean? Does that mean to order in? Does that mean you'll look after yourself or others for that meal? Does that mean to thaw and microwave something? Does that mean to plan a meal and make it all from basic staple ingredients? Does that mean to pay for the bill at a restaurant? Phrases can be even more complex than single words. So, we must begin with defining the terms.

Many parents and families do not discuss the difference between rules and expectations. The vast majority of expectations are never clearly articulated. While rules for safety such as a curfew may have been very clear, expectations are not typically as clear. They are communicated through vague conversation and reinforced through behavior.

## An Example:

When I first started high school, I had always been a good student. Starting at a new school in a new town, I struggled with the teaching method. As a result, I brought home my first report card with a D on it. My mother put it on the fridge and stated that there would be no entertainment until that grade was acceptable. Now, to me, that felt like a punishment for violating a rule that I wasn't sure had been articulated to me. In reality, the results of my efforts had not met with expectations. The violation of those expectations resulted in, not a conversation about expectations or difficulties with the transition, but precipitated a punishment, typically reserved for broken rules. Understand this is not an admonishment of my parents, but rather an illustration of how parents and children perceive things very differently.

If you revisit your list of rules, how many were actually not rules, but expectations? Quickly, it becomes clear that not everything listed was a rule, but perhaps was perceived as a rule. Expectations carry with them a bundle of emotional issues. In many respects, this is where many first learn about failure.

Consider that we don't fail if we break a rule, we must have decided to break that rule. But violating an expectation is where we begin to understand what it means to not measure up, to be less than what we are supposed to be, to have failed to meet a goal in some respect. We learn quickly that violating expectations at best disappoints others. How we as individuals deal with failure is often created at this very early stage of not really even understanding what the expectations are. In this process we learn shame and self-loathing. Why? Because we are not what others want or expect us to be. The expectations of others that dominate our own existence often rob us of our own ideas, identity, desires, and expectations. Expectations can also destroy relationships if they are not articulated.

Consider the effect of expectations. If we go to the doctor with a list of symptoms, we expect the doctor to listen, explore, and then recommend a treatment. If the doctor prescribes a placebo, we still expect the prescription to work, and in most cases, it does. The power of expectation alters our own perception of reality. When was the last time you had expectations and what did that mean?

## But what about family culture?

Still again, some of the listed rules may not be rules, but family culture. When we are born, we carry no rules, no expectations, and no family culture. We learn these things; a lot of times through trial and error. Imagine that when you are born, you are born into a clear bubble in which you exist. This bubble becomes the place where we store experiences and information. We learn early that if we cry, we will gain the attention of those that care for us. We learn many powerful lessons through experience such as that the stove is hot. Pain is a powerful deterrent. As we grow, we add experiences, like little post it notes on the inside of that bubble. We document things like when we receive presents, when people sleep, when to hold hands, don't spit out food, when we eat food, who sleeps where, and so many other things. But each of these may be quite different depending on the family.

Family culture is different than expectations as family culture is made up of the collage of rules, expectations, relationships, and the changing dynamic of all of these things changing with time. The best way to examine this concept is to consider a family holiday like Christmas, Chanukah, or Eid. There are rules and some of the rules are determined by an external cultural influence such as religion. But some of the rules are determined by how a particular family interprets those rules and implements them. Similarly, there are expectations of culture, religion, and still separate again, expectations of family and self.

Finally, there is family culture which may be quite different from the dominant culture, from the religious culture and from popular culture. My sister once told me that she valued family because they're the only ones who truly understand our particular brand of crazy. So true. I grew up in urban California and rural North Dakota and Minnesota. I grew up walking between two very different cultures. My grandparents all grew up in southern rural areas with a profound Christian belief system. My mother made our clothes. My father insisted on academic excellence. My mother loves to make things from food to sewing to stained glass. My father loves toys and to read and learn. I understand, from two very different worlds, the value placed on family provenance. I have a strange childlike appreciation of joy and simple things like coloring, cooking, or sewing. I enjoy making my own things and projects rather than buying things in the store. While I value family identity, there is no one place I have ever called home; until now. I am as comfortable at a cattle branding as I am at a California Gala fundraiser. This is the intersection between family culture and expectation.

How many of the rules were not really rules, but family culture?

But why is this important? In nearly 30 years of asking this question on the first day of class I've learn that this is not something most have examined. As adults, their first responsibility is to begin to manage their own lives and that includes creating their own rules, expectations, and culture. It is also important to realize that the box in which we find ourselves may not be of our own making, but only we can destroy it. It is essential in relationships to understand that everyone comes with their own set of rules, expectations, and culture. Exploring these elements are the building blocks of a sound relationship.

I have had students realize they were pursuing the degree their parents expected or in line with the family business or culture, but not aligned with their own desires. I have had students realize they were pursuing a life that their parents wanted them to have and not at all what they would want for themselves.

I have seen employees in a corporate environment realize they were placing personal rules and expectations inappropriately on their coworkers. I have seen managers realize that they became managers because that was the family expectation and that they actually preferred creative work over managerial work.

# CHAPTER 2

# Semantics

*Activity #2:*
Please write a detailed response to the question. Considering what we now understand about rules, expectations, and family culture; what are the rules at work or at school? Perhaps consider the rules, expectations and family culture surrounding relationships.

## Rules, Expectations, and Family Culture

After two weeks of class Jon came to chat with me after class. He had just realized that the aviation degree he was pursuing was not for him. After some consideration of rules, expectations and culture; he figured out that the expectations of that life were not in line with his passion. He was interested in computers and education.

It was incredibly complicated for Jon to switch majors. He had already incurred a huge debt load from flying. Now, he would be switching colleges, essentially starting over as a freshman. Not a financially wise thing to do, but it meant he would likely be much more successful and happier with his pursuits. He switched his major to business; entrepreneurship specifically and began exploring ventures that would marry computers and education.

He came to me a couple weeks later with an idea to build custom computers. I told him to go do the research; who was doing this now and what did it take to be successful at it. He came back disappointed after discovering that someone else had already built the system he had envisioned and was now mass producing it. But he had another idea as a result. Turns out making prototypes is incredibly expensive in North Dakota. Jon happened upon the idea of 3D printing prototypes as a way of proving a concept. He launched 3C Innovations and began 3D printing prototypes and advising schools on how they could incorporate 3D printing into their curriculum to enhance learning. Jon ran 3C Innovations for four years until he started his master's program in instructional design. Jon focused on how to build out enhanced, engaging, and experiential computer learning models in higher education.

Jon's struggle was not in discovering that he didn't actually want to be a pilot. The struggle was that he had spent years justifying the expectation and now had to build an entirely different expectation for himself. That conversation about delayed graduation and increased student debt undoubtedly caused some tensions in his relationships. It requires extensive conversations and the adjustment of the expectations of others.

## Personally:

As a child every adult I knew had a job and another job. What do I mean by this? My father was a middle school English teacher but was also a minister. My mother pursued a day job and then side projects such as design work. My stepfather worked for the federal government, but also owned and managed an apartment building and a cable company. My grandfather was a minister and enjoyed being a laborer. No one in my immediate family had one job, but rather worked hard all the time and loved it! If there was time in the day, you could be working. Therefore, according to the perspective on rules, expectations, and family culture, it was my family culture to work hard and be productive at all times. The expectation was that at a very young age we would all begin to work and earn our own way and that as adults we would also not only have a primary job, but a secondary job and always be productive. This, in the mind of a child turns into rules and the rules told this child that life was work, so work hard, be productive at all times, sitting still is sinful, and laziness has a price.

Quickly, you can see how this might create difficulties in relationships not only personal but at work. I started my first business at 15 cleaning houses and local businesses. I did not hang out with friends much but worked. In college, I carried a load of 21 credits each semester and held down a job as well as secured a scholarship for speech and debate. I had never learned what to do with "free time" except to find work and be productive. I never learned the art of idle chit chat at work. And as I began to date and consider a life with someone, it was clear that my work ethic was a problem. Others called me a workaholic, but in all honesty, I wasn't addicted to work or success, but I grew up in a dynamic where this was normal. My box was made of expectations of work and success.

My husband and sons for years have told me I'm incapable of sitting still. I simply tell people I'm not very good at it. I don't sit still well. I enjoy projects. I enjoy maintaining my home. I enjoy cooking for others. I enjoy walking. I enjoy karate. I do not enjoy television. If I do watch something I am also sewing or knitting. Finally, I am learning to slow down, but not much.

Sometimes, it is not us that must adjust our behaviors but others. Recently, my husband said he was spending a day doing absolutely nothing. But soon, an idea struck him for a project. He could no longer sit still and do nothing. He tried to fight the impulse, but simply could not and began to draw designs for the project and tidy the area to make room for that project. Then in an off handed comment he told me he had caught my disease as he just could not do nothing. I believe we've found a happy medium. I have learned to slow down and do things WITH my family and they have learned that they can initiate on projects and find ways to build a better life.

## At Work:

Rules, expectations, and culture also apply broadly to work. The rules of work are also often safety related. Hard hats, work boots, safety glasses, ergonomic chairs and keyboards, fire drills, training, and security measures are all rules as a result of safety or risk mitigation. I did not include time in this list because this is where the rules are shifting into expectation. Many grew up in an era of a set work time to clock in and clock out. Punching the clock meant inserting your timecard into a mechanized device that would punch or stamp the time on your timecard both as you began and ended work. Punching the clock was accompanied by certain policies that are also not rules. Policies stated things like if you are late you will be paid for the next time segment but not before which means you may lose pay for clocking in late. But policies are not rules.

Arriving early is an expectation, but not necessarily a rule. In many cultures staying late is also an expectation, but not a rule. While most employers are required to provide a lunch break and other breaks, many do not enforce this rule and therefore expect employees to either take those breaks on their own or to eat lunch at their desks or while still working. The expectation used to be that all employees should be 15 minutes early. But this also came with the employee expectation that they would receive breaks. This culture is changing to be more fluid. While you may be asked to participate in a meeting over lunch, you also are expected to still remain until the end of the business day. Some organizations use an even more fluid expectation of time by allowing employees to work from home or to adjust their schedule to come in later and work later or arrive earlier and leave earlier.

Expectations may shift without notice as managers or supervisors move and shift. Managers establish expectations through consistent feedback on behaviors and performance. But if a new manager is introduced into the system, the expectations must be established and discussed. The incoming manager must realize that old expectations exist, they must be assessed, addressed, and discussed before changes occur or employees grow mistrustful.

Each workplace also has a culture like family has a culture. Ideo, a well-known creative firm, has a culture of openness and creativity. The founders expect that employees will bring up ideas that conflict with their ideas. But this conflict is not met with expectation violation or behavior correction. Rather it is embraced as excellent communication and creativity.

Other corporate cultures may be quite closed and limiting. Having experienced negative feedback from contributing openly, employees may retort that a request is above their pay grade, implying a strict hierarchy within the culture. The corporate culture may be competitive or cooperative, creative or productive, profit driven or mission driven. Understanding the corporate culture and the box it creates for us is just as important as understanding family culture and the box it creates.

Consider for a moment a workplace in another country. I was invited to teach at the University of Shanghai for Science and Technology first in 2016 and then again in 2018. After teaching two terms in Shanghai, China, the differences in the culture of higher education, the rules of families, and the expectations of employers, families and friends became clearer. Western higher education has rules around plagiarism. If you didn't write it, cite it. But other cultures don't think this way. If you learned it, you earned it; it belongs to you now. This profound difference in culture has tremendous implications in applications of rules in higher education. The entire dynamic of the classroom in China demonstrated that Western and Eastern concepts of cooperation and classroom culture are very different. In the West, many educators take attendance utilizing swipe cards or online log ins. Each student is responsible for their own attendance and tracking that attendance is the responsibility of the faculty member. However, during my time in China, a student "monitor" was assigned to take attendance. But quickly I noticed that there were more names on the attendance sheet than were actually in the room. When I asked my teaching assistant (the dean) about this he said that some will write down the name of someone they know is not in attendance, but that in doing so they are taking responsibility for that absent person and their understanding of the material. A student in charge of taking attendance and student taking responsibility for the learning of other students; these are foreign concepts to Western education indeed.

The physical culture of education was also dramatically different. The classrooms were not heated and students often kept their coats on during class or cradled bottles of hot water or tea. A bell rang loudly every hour signaling a break. Classes must halt giving everyone a break then resume when the second bell rings, rather like Western public school systems. There were no photocopy services and no reams of paper available. There was no computer in my office as I was expected to supply my own. If I wanted a quiz photocopied, I had to provide the paper. The dean of the college was my teaching assistant; a profound departure from the function of a dean in the West. The dean was charged with ensuring that the visiting professors had all they needed and while classroom instruction was delivered in English, the dean was also there to clarify if needed and to ensure that the visiting professor understood the culture and policies of the institution. Every classroom was monitored via closed circuit cameras. My office was a luxury office as it featured a small heater. The teaching building and the faculty office building were separate on campus. Faculty office doors were kept closed and hallway conversations were discouraged as unproductive. Instead, faculty would go for walks together or enjoy a meal together promoting collegiality and working on projects or research in this way. Umbrellas were kept open in the hallway so they would dry. The bathroom was a BYOTP situation (Bring your own toilet paper). The faculty believed that resources should be dedicated only to things that will promote the institution and student learning. The cleaning staff would gather on a grassy spot and use old t-shirts to create mops with bamboo handles. Their jobs demanded that they provide their own cleaning supplies. Nothing else is essential.

Rules, expectations, and culture all play vital roles in how we function and think, but that may be part of the problem.

## Where the Rules, Expectations, and Culture Conflict: Politics

I do not do politics well. I just don't see how an alternative and hidden agenda is helpful. How could the manipulation of other people be viewed as professional? And yet, politics continue in the workplace. Office politics is the intersection of rules/policies, expectations, and culture. We go to work and learn the policies or rules. We are sometimes told the expectations and we learn the culture. But sometimes, these three things are in conflict.

Years ago, I assisted a manager at work. Often, she would come into my office with a situation and we would talk through options openly and creatively. Later, I would hear my words come from her mouth. I didn't think anything of it until sometime later I created a mentorship program. When the program was praised by upper management, I found my manager took credit for the idea and the program. People around me who knew how the program had been developed were insistent that I say something. I saw no reason to. Ideas have no value unless they are acted upon. Idea ownership is even more difficult to cultivate and understand.

In my next position, again, I had open conversations with my manager. I coordinated several interns conducting their final projects needed for graduation. There was little information available from previous iterations. I contacted other programs at the university and suggested we get all the internship coordinators together to discuss best practices. Within two years I had established a regularly meeting group of all faculty that utilized internships or cooperatives in their programs and we had realigned all our programs to meet industry, university, state and federal government standards to protect student workers. However, in a program review with my boss's boss, my boss took credit for the group and the changes.

Years later, at another institution, I decided no one would take credit for my work. I documented feverishly and launched ideas independently. I built several programs including an entrepreneur coach position that saw a young entrepreneur use our office space as their physical address, our computers and resources for their business in exchange for coaching new ideas into a more feasible shape before actual venture coaching could occur. I also started building a student investment fund that would be operated entirely by students for students. My manager chastised me at MY board meeting. He stated that I do excellent work, but that I don't collaborate enough.

In my next position, I was open and honest with my manager about this particular issue. She was very understanding and from the very beginning, we established a system where people with the ideas got the credit and who ever worked on the project also got the credit, but the final accolades always went to the program as a whole.

Most recently, I created a summer research institute. Students would work directly with me to do qualitative rhetorical research. I put everything in place including the interview protocols, the institutional ethics review, and even selected the students and secured a grant. When the research began, I was fired. I learned that management had checked on the research to see if they would own it if I was gone. Indeed, they would, but ONLY the data mentioned in the documents. I had learned a valuable lesson from the past. I knew no one in the program understood qualitative rhetorical research. I knew that the data would be meaningless without the education; my PhD. They can have the raw data, but they won't know how to extract the necessary information nor publish the findings without me. I left out key elements; the secret sauce.

This is politics. It is the manipulation of people for the purposes of power. People use the rules and policies against expectation and functionality in order to appear more creative or productive than they actually are. This same theme seems to happen wherever I go. My friends and family insist that I not "give away" ideas anymore. But why would I hold back creativity that is needed just because credit is given elsewhere?

The problem is that I have established the expectation that my ideas will not remain mine nor will I receive the credit for them. When someone mentions these ideas in meetings claiming ownership, I do not correct the individual. In allowing this to continue, I devalue the idea and the work involved in creating the idea.

Here's where rules or workplace policies such as authority and respectful workplace conflict with expectations of both managers and employees. Managers expect that the policies will be followed. By creating open and creative conversations, the managers understand they can take credit for ideas or programs and the employees are powerless to do anything about it without flying in the face of policy. Then again, if I withhold ideas, I violate their and my expectations for a creative and open work environment. Many companies or higher education institutions claim to be creative and open. Companies try to reframe themselves by chanting the buzz words like creative and open or innovative and fluid. People persuade themselves that it's about the work, but then harbor hurt feelings and misgivings. Violations such as this happen once, then ideas are withheld and productivity decreases.

Rules, expectations and culture are rarely in sync. They usually conflict. Culture may not abide by the rules as some things are overlooked because they work but are against the rules. Consider how long there have been harassment regulations in workplaces, and yet, only recently have workplace cultures begun to align with those regulations. People experienced harassment or watched it but did nothing because it could cost them their jobs. For years, many individuals continued to create uncomfortable work environments because the rules and the culture were misaligned. The rules may demand some form of reporting of mistreatment, but the culture strongly urges everyone to "just get along" or to be "thicker skinned."

Employers may expect more than the rules state that can actually be against the common culture. Consider employment that requires overtime but does not pay it. This practice continues and is often masked in salaried positions. Or individuals are encouraged to "work from home" to try to balance the workload. In these cases, many people feel they are being bullied or targeted. The conflict of these three things always results turmoil.

Many years ago, it was common where I was teaching to teach five or six sections of 45 students. The faculty began to feel the strain. We advocated for smaller class sizes or fewer classes. But the institution claimed that the workload was our own fault. If we just did multiple choice, we could then use scantron to grade.

If we just did midterms and finals, we could manage the work-load just fine. But as professionals, we knew that would greatly jeopardize the quality of education and leave many students failing who did not test well under multiple choice restrictions. Besides, we were the applied knowledge institution and it is difficult to demonstrate applied knowledge through multiple choice. The conflict seemed to fly in the face of what was widely touted as the ethos of the institution. The culture did not match the rules or expectations.

# CHAPTER 3

# Promises

*Activity #3:*

Take a moment and list all the promises you've made and those that others have made to you. Take notice that they may not have been actual verbal promises but are implied in relationships. Consider things like wedding vows or bargains we have made with friends.

This activity tends to be a little more difficult. We often don't think about the promises we make. We often make them without consideration. We tell a friend "Whatever you do, don't drink and drive. Call me and I'll come get you." That's a promise. That's a bargain struck out of concern. This is typically where the list begins but it's hard to remember the promises and see them as separate from expectations.

But if we back up, and instead of listing all the promises, we begin with a list of the people in our lives, then the task becomes somewhat easier. Perhaps a list of your friends reveals that you made them a promise to always be there for them. That becomes a challenge in adulthood as people move and make lives of their own or have families.

As a college student, I joined Kappa Alpha Theta. I made several promises to them the least of which was to guard the secrets of the organization. Perhaps as an athlete you signed a scholarship contract; a promise to maintain a certain grade point average. Perhaps as a young person you signed a morality pledge. Perhaps when you tested for your driver's license you signed a don't text and drive promise.

We make a lot of promises without a lot of thought. I promised a lot of people I would always be there for them, not realizing that at any moment I could be hit by a bus. I do try to keep that promise through technology. But it's often not the same.

Don't panic if this activity is quite difficult. I have found that about half of the people who have done this activity find it quite challenging. They didn't realize how often they make promises without thinking. When we buy a large ticket item like a car, we sign a promissory note; a promise to pay. When we enter into an exclusive relationship, we often make a promise of fidelity.

When we marry, we make a lot of promises and a lot of people don't even remember their vows years later. We make promises to our children. We make promises to our parents. We make promises to deities

Here's the real kicker, we make a lot of promises to ourselves. The truly sad thing is that when things get busy, those are often the first promises we break. We promise ourselves we will eat healthy. We promise ourselves we will exercise. We promise ourselves to make time for relaxation. We promise ourselves that we will never let anyone take advantage of us. We promise ourselves to be true to our own nature. We promise ourselves that someday....

We seem to hold ourselves more to promises we make to other people, than the promises we make to ourselves. We often use the term "promise" very lightly and dismissively. But a promise is the foundational step to rules, expectations and culture. We may even have made promises without even knowing it. We may have made promises in our youth that we can't possibly keep in adulthood. We may have made promises that it would not be prudent to keep.

Once we have discussed all the promises we make, three things tend to happen with this activity. There's a group of people that realize they have untidy promise practices and they often spend a great deal of time contemplating this. There's a group that due to their youth or lifestyle, simply have made very few promises. Then there's the group that realizes that it's time to make significant changes to their list of promises and how they make promises.

Untidy promises mean that we have made a lot of promises that have expiration dates or conditions. Or perhaps just with life and culture we realize these promises change. We make promises in the heat of a moment, steeped in emotion but when the emotion is diluted, we quietly rescind the promise. Many begin to realize that they are not blameless victims in the rules, expectations and culture. They realize they actually acknowledged the necessary promises to make those things happen. But again, after a week of deeply contemplating the nature of their promises, this group goes back to old behaviors and rarely stops to think about the promises they've made.

Relationships and connections occur over time and become solidified through common experience. When we are young, there are very few of those connections. But as we grow and experience more, we also create more of those connections. We go out and do something with friends, then make a promise to never tell a soul. How many times have we begun a sentence "Between you and me...." That's a promise of confidence. Do we keep our confidences? How many times do we say "I owe you one" then promptly forget. The second group don't see the promises they've made. It's hard to find the actual promise among the day to day of life and friendship or family.

Finally, there's a group of participants that realizes they've been taking the term and practice of "promise" very lightly. They begin to change their rhetoric surrounding these kinds of agreements. They are very deliberate in wording and specific in details. This group also begins to bring the attention of others to the rhetoric of promises. They say things like "Don't promise what you can't deliver" or "Is that a promise or a threat" or perhaps "my mouth made a promise my body couldn't keep."

We must all realize that people think about promises very differently. To make a promise off-handedly or dismissively may alter a relationship forever. It can be very difficult to understand how someone else views promises. In family life, promising to clean your room after just one more game is dangerous. Promises like this are often forgotten and only made to ensure they can indeed play one more game and that the interrupting person will go away. Perhaps we are lining up our activities for the day and someone asks us to add to that list. We say yes, but somewhere along the line we forget in the busy parts of the list.

Promises are broken. Just look at the current divorce rate and we know that even the most sacred of promises are broken. Smaller promises are broken daily. Many marriage vows include things like "Love, honor, and keep him/her in sickness and health, richer or poorer, until death us do part." We get the love part. But do we get the honor part? Do we understand the keep part?

We break promises to ourselves most often. How can we expect others to trust our promises when we often make promises to ourselves that we know we won't keep? We make promises to institutions like banks. We make promises to end conversations.

## Examples:

My youngest son, when he was very small, maybe 4 years old, promised his Dad he would chew his food for him if he lost all his teeth. As disgusting as that sounds, it was a loving promise to care for him in his old age. That promise still comes up now and again, but it's brought up dismissively like a joke or something cute a small child does. And yet, the expectation remains that our children will care for us in our twilight years.

The office of President comes with a swearing in. The President, after elected, but before they can execute any official duties, must swear to "Faithfully execute the office of President of the United States and will to the best of my ability, preserve, protect and defend the Constitution of the United States." But here's the rub, nowhere does it mention the people of the US. Nowhere does it mention right or wrong. The office of the President takes an oath or promise to defend a document.

## Section Review and Work

1) The rules you live by may not have been made by you. As an adult, it's time to examine those rules and determine which serve your purposes and which do not.

2) Expectations can be dangerous. Children do not differentiate rules from expectations and learn failure through violating expectations, not by breaking rules. Consider the expectations in your life, where do they come from and do they serve you?

3) Family culture can be the cumulative sum of rules and expectations seasoned with cultural influences such as religion or gender roles. However, as adults we begin to build our own culture through our relationships and passions. The first step toward understanding family culture is to determine the norms.

4) How many of the rules of your youth follow you today?

5) What expectations do you hold for yourself? What expectations do you still carry for others?

6) How has family culture impacted your relationships or choices in work or education?

7) Beginning this work allows us to see the basic outline of the box we live in and that a lot of that box was not of our own making. In considering and perhaps eliminating

some of the rules, expectations, and cultural elements, we can begin to break down the box that confines us.

8) Consider the rules, expectations, and culture at work or school. How do they align or conflict?

9) What promises do you make and keep?

# PART TWO

---

## Breaking Out and Breaking Through

DAILY SPECIALS

| Yesterday | Today | Tommorow |
|-----------|-------|----------|
| Fish | Routine | WTF Fusion |
| Baked | Poutine | Flambe |
| Potato | Average | Left Field |
| Soup | Alfredo | Linguine |
| Salad | Run of the | Sea Cucumber |
| | Mill | Quesdilla |
| | Ravioli | |

# CHAPTER 4

# The Adventure Begins

*Activity #4:*
This is a standing assignment I give all my students. This week do something you've never done before. It doesn't have to be dramatic like sky diving. But do something you've never done. Take a different route to work, try a new recipe, sit with different people at lunch, the possibilities are endless.

The college experience for most is a vast departure from the familiar. Most students are on their own for the first time. Dorm living, joining a Greek letter organization, apartment living all demand students do new things. Even if students are living at home while attending college, new experiences are a daily occurrence. But it is often the case that these are overlooked or seen as an inconvenience. Few view this opportunity as just that; an opportunity. Students strive to keep a lot of their pre-college routine in place with the same friends, the same workouts, the same job, even the same schedule.

In the corporate environment, many strive for routine management. Leaders attempt to keep things the same and often discourage new pursuits or ideas. As leaders it is important to remember what striving means and the benefit of experiencing the unfamiliar regularly. Seeking out new things to do and experience can produce an environment where change is welcomed and expected instead of managed and difficult.

At the beginning of each class I ask my students to report on what they did that week that they'd never done before. At first no one wants to report. Then there's a brave soul that raises their hand and reports that they wandered around a different building or took a new route to class. Some may report they went to the gym for the first time or perhaps a new exercise regimen. If they didn't do something new, I spend a couple minutes with them brainstorming what they might do. Taking it one step further, I ask them to form groups and make a plan to do something together that none of them has done.

It's funny how we cling to the old, the familiar, the tried and true or the broken but whatever. It seems like such a simple assignment, but the results are surprising. There are typically three responses.

First, there's the group of students that embrace this assignment as an excuse to do the things they've been wanting to. Some start very small like walking a different route to class or sitting in a different seat. There's a strange classroom culture that seems to be an elementary school holdover that sees students sitting in the same seats even without assigned seating. Some do something more dramatic like try a new restaurant or join a new sports group. Some have even taken up music lessons or booked a vacation. This group is happy to participate, eager for the change and excitement of the adventure. They are often the ones that drag others into the assignment. They discover new activities, new places on campus, hidden gems of history within the community, new interests or games, and find out that doing something new is often the key to distressing and improving creativity.

Among corporate participants, this first group tends to start to brag about their new adventures, the grander the better. They begin to relate their new-found hobby of doing things they've never done before to work situations. For example, how do new customers find our business? How can we decrease the uncertainty of trying something new or how can we make trying something new more exciting?

Second, there's the group that reluctantly tries a new thing or two. They may try a new food or a new Netflix series. Their adventures are relatively safe. They don't venture too far from their comfort zone. They rarely attempt something that they cannot predict the outcome. New food is fairly easy to try and if you don't like it you have only had one bite, maybe. Netflix tells you how long an episode is so you can predict how long the activity will take. Also, Netflix recommends things to you based on previous viewing. Similarly, Netflix allows the viewer to stop something their watching at any time and rate it so they can prevent future similar shows from appearing on their list. It's a pretty safe bet either way. But they soon get pulled into the excitement of the first group and through this, larger groups are formed that begin to do things together. The second group realizes they could do more or be more adventurous, but they still seek the safety of companions. They will conspire and put together a group to do something like an escape room, intramural sports, or a guest speaker. There's a safety in numbers that this group needs that the first group doesn't.

In a corporate environment, this group tends to examine what keeps people feeling safe. They focus on not sparking interest, but guarantees, free trials, or no penalty free opting out.

Finally, there's the group that refuses to do this activity. Their lives are just fine, thank you. They enjoy their routine. They enjoy the safety of the known and predictable. Trying something new takes time and energy they don't wish to divert from what they are already doing. Taking a new route to class may mean they are late and they value being on time and the predictability of their route over the adventure of a new one. They enjoy their small circle of friends. Those friends are predictable and stable. The awkward getting to know you phase can be avoided. They watch reruns and enjoy remembering particular episodes. They enjoy trivia and being content experts. But what they do learn is that there are things in the world they are refusing to do BECAUSE they have never done them. They begin to realize that what they are doing now is exactly what their life will be forever without doing something new and different. However, this also comes with tremendous comfort.

In a corporate setting, this group values tradition, stability, and predictability. They value systems and processes. They tend to emphasize the longevity of the company or product. They communicate to customers and employees the value of doing things in a traditional way with years of experience.

I've gotten to the point where I do this routinely, sometimes daily. I don't even think about it anymore. As a matter of fact, when I'm asked about what I've done recently that I've never done before I have to stop and think because doing new things has become routine. I dropped off fresh produce from my garden to at a student's house, anonymously. Today, I'm lounging on the couch at my sister's home in California working in the warm sun rather than at my home in frigid Manitoba. I frequently seek out new recipes. I make a point of trying new apps on my mobile device once a month. But even doing something new every day or week becomes a habit.

If driving and finding construction or a detour throws off your day, then this activity will definitely benefit you. If you find yourself looking for something new to try as you stare at the same food stuffs in your pantry, you guessed it, this is a great activity for you. There are websites where you can put in your ingredients and they will provide you with recipes and ideas. Try a new podcast, a new app, a new machine at the gym. The possibilities are endless.

It is this spirit of adventure that will serve you well through this book. Embrace doing new things. Embrace the unknown. Embrace subtle changes.

## An Example:

As a professor, I frequently invite in guest speakers. The students research the individual before they speak and come armed with questions. One such speaker, Pam, from a small community told the story of how she was upset and decided to "just drive around." While doing this she found herself taking routes and roads she hadn't in likely a decade or more. That's hard to do in a small community of 60,000. As she was driving, she noticed a large retail space was emptying out. The space was fantastic; access from the road, good parking, huge potential for multiple uses. She put the thought aside and continued with her day. But the opportunities for that space kept interrupting her day. She finally phoned the owners to find out what was going on with the space. Turns out they were retiring and were going to sell the real estate.

Pam made an offer. She knew the offer was low, but she just couldn't get the flood of ideas to stop after she'd seen them emptying the space. She did buy the real estate and opened first a carpet store, then added lighting, then added all kinds of unique décor often featuring local artisans. As an entrepreneur, Pam had had many successes, but this turned out to be her biggest success. She credits it all to random driving.

## Make a list:

Use this space to make a list of new things you could do. This isn't a "bucket list" or a list of things you want to do before you die. It's merely a list of ideas, easily accessible things you could do each day that you've never done before.

# CHAPTER 5

# New People

*Activity #5:*
Each day this week find two strangers
to talk to. Start a conversation!

I get it, we are told to NOT talk to strangers. But if we never meet anyone new then we will have the social circle we have right now for the rest of our lives. It becomes critical to talk to strangers. Students actually do this quite well. After all, most of their classes include strangers and then there's that dreaded activity; group work! The occupation of being a student requires them to talk to strangers. Students talk to new professors, classmates, librarians, dining services workers, financial officers, housing administrators, advisors, and countless more. But we can take this one step further. We can be intentional about starting conversations. We can talk to the clerk in the store or the other people in line. We can talk to people waiting for the bus.

By the way, giving your order to a server you don't know or asking the bus driver about the next stop, doesn't count. You have to actually engage in conversation. You need to learn their name and at least one bit of information about them not related to the activity in which you find yourselves.

The art of conversation is dying. As we utilize more and more technology, not actually communicating through that channel to people we already know replaying the same conversations in a bizarre loop, we forget what it's like to actually learn about people and meet new people. Conversation used to be taught as a subject in schools. Specifically finishing schools would offer courses in conversation.

Some students embrace this activity understanding that networking is an essential skill. Most occupations require that you speak to strangers. During this session, participants brainstorm new ways to start conversations. Figuring out how to talk to strangers is often the most difficult part. How do you start a conversation with a total stranger without it sounding weird or creepy? We have become so entrenched in our technology rich world that we forget that people for centuries had to talk to strangers daily. Conversation was entertainment! At first, it will be awkward, but with practice, most people become quite adept at starting conversations. Keeping those conversations going, however, is another topic.

I tell my students to start simple. I've found three quick and easy ways to start conversations with anyone.

1) Start by commenting on something you notice and use a compliment like "I really love your jacket! Where did you get it?" Talking about something like clothing is often not all that personal and people typically easily share this kind of information. Be sincere and ask a question to which you really want to know the answer to. "I love your car! How do you take care of it?" But be careful about verging on the creepy. "I love your car, what's in the glove box?" Rather than starting with a random person, perhaps start with someone who is paid to talk to you like your coffee barista or the grocery store clerk. Ask them what they recommend on the menu and why? Ask them the best time to come in when it's not so busy? Ask them the most bizarre thing someone has ordered. The conversation can blossom from there.

2) Second, you can ask for assistance. You may not actually need help, but sometimes, it's just a good way to start a conversation. "I wonder if you can help me find my class-room?" "Sorry to disturb you, but I wonder if you could show me how to use this machine?" This works well at the gym or when traveling. Many places have kiosks for train tickets or other travel. "Would you happen to know when the next bus downtown is due?" Again, you can start with people paid to talk to you. Ask the person at the

deli counter that you want to try something new (2 birds approach) and ask them to recommend something. Ask a librarian to recommend a book. Ask a caretaker about the hidden wonders on campus.

3) Finally, you can always offer assistance or company. "Here, let me get the door for you." That's just courteous. "Can I help you with your books?" These are either statements or binary questions (yes or no). To start a conversation, you'll have to venture into open ended questions. It's a common practice in China to sit with strangers at a meal. Ask the new hire in your office if they have any questions or if they just want to have coffee.

But the conversation can't end there. Show some gratitude, say thank you. Tell them you are making a point of meeting people and ask their name. Honesty is always a great approach. I often tell students to throw me under the bus and say, "I have this crazy professor that makes us meet new people, would you mind terribly being my homework?" Better yet, combine the last two activities and say something like "Hi, I'm sorry to disturb you, but I have this crazy professor that wants us to find new things to do. I wonder if you could give me a couple ideas about new things you've tried recently." You spoke to a stranger and maybe got some ideas of new things you might try.

## Examples:

I stood in the grocery line many years ago as a woman stood in front of me with some stunning jewelry. I had decided I needed to improve my conversational skills and had set the goal of speaking to strangers. I asked her where she got the jewelry. Turns out she owned a store that featured new artists and the jewelry was from a new collection. We started chatting and exchanged business cards. During that brief conversation we discovered we had several common interests. She had just left Nortel, a disastrous end to a tech company had found her entertaining her entrepreneurial side. She wanted to start a women's only gym in the area next and I was looking for just such a place to work out. We worked together on the project and a year later she opened Image Fitness. All this sprouted from a chance conversation in the grocery store.

I get it, conversations require a small amount of trust. We don't trust strangers easily. In our own communities we may not trust the person across the street. When traveling we may find we trust people we encounter who are from our region.

We loved our time in Shanghai. We explored whenever we could. We would make daily plans about where we would go after I was done with work. We made lists and gathered maps for our explorations. But living abroad for any length of time can be isolating. We were looking for something a little familiar. A former student who had also travelled in Shanghai recommended The Boxing Cat. We had been wandering for about 30 minutes with our hotel map in hand trying to find The Boxing Cat. After all, it was a restaurant recommended by a friend so we couldn't just give up. Navigating Shanghai was no easy feat. But we finally found the place and had settled in to enjoy a couple beverages. Some areas of Shanghai have a high tourist population so non-Asian individuals don't particularly stand out. But in this area of Shanghai, there were very few non-Asian visitors indeed. At the table next to us sat a Western looking man enjoying a beer. As he had already ordered, I asked him what he had ordered and if he was enjoying it. After a brief conversation about his beverage and meal choice, we discovered that he was in Shanghai visiting his parents who also frequently taught abroad. He was from Sacramento, where I was born, and we exchanged some of the sights we had each visited complete with navigation. Unlike the previous example, this didn't become a lifelong friend or colleague. Actually, we never saw him again. But we did learn of two places we decided to visit thanks to that conversation.

# CHAPTER 6

# Observe Deeply

*Activity #6:*

This activity is more fun if you involve a few people. Select a place to spend some time. Take a notebook. Observe everything from the traffic on the way there, access to the parking lot, the number of spaces, plants or landscaping, signage, lighting, and frontage. Observe everything. You should end up with at least 10 pages of notes. Include diagrams.

We go places all the time, but we rarely invest our time and energy in observing where we are. We know the menu but can't remember the color of the carpet. We know the weekly specials, but never noticed the chairs don't match. The server knows your order, but you don't know his name.

As participants arrive, I ask them to select a group, a small group. I then ask them to select a place they've all been and recall as much as they can about the place. After 20 minutes, most believe they have written down all there is. They then go to the place and observe EVERYTHING.

Students always enjoy leaving the classroom. They also enjoy the chance to go hang out as an assignment.

When students return to the classroom or participants to the boardroom, they buzz with all the things they had never noticed before. Like most group work, there's a group that does the minimum. They go to a fast food joint and comment on how plastic, loud, and generally greasy everything was. They forget everything that has come before in the class. They forget to examine how they know where the line is, how to order, what to get and what not to get, and how to pay. They forget the culture of the place and the rules as the expectations take over. They forget that the expectation of mass standardization is paramount. In a corporate setting, these individuals often overlook key differences not observing whether the kitchen is visible or not, whether there's a drive thru or not, or how the food is delivered or not. Painting all similar establishments with the same colors and brush, they miss the subtle differences that create loyal customers such as Coke or Pepsi or flame broiled or fried.

But some groups embrace the assignment. After this activity, they begin to see a lot of things they never noticed before. They begin to observe, put down their mobile device and really observe. After doing something new each week and talking to strangers as well as examining rules and expectations, participants begin to see that activities such as these can build on each other. They talk to the employees. They eavesdrop on other customers. They order something they've never had. They seek differences and similarities. They examine pictures, greetings, prices, bathrooms, seating, windows, advertisements, play areas. Better yet, they go somewhere they've only been to a few times and really challenge themselves. They may even notice condiments on the table or the manner in which customers use the available amenities such as play facilities or outdoor seating. In a corporate environment, these participants automatically select things that will also aid them in their own employment such as price comparisons, service models, charitable contributions, cleaning schedules, communicated competitor differences, happy employees, or better yet, considering what would the extra mile be in this situation and what would be the competitive advantage or disadvantage. They examine parking, access from the road, lighting in the parking lot or inside, the ceiling, the floor, the furniture, the "extras" or lack thereof, the language culture created for that particular establishment and so much more.

Businesses open and close all the time. Entrepreneurs are so excited to just get started they forget to do real research on a location. Entrepreneurs often think about the square footage or the rent but rarely take in all the information or observe how people interact with the space they hope to occupy. Participants begin to appreciate detailed observational research.

## An Example

At the age of 51, I've been training in Shotokan Karate for about 16 years. I had acquired advanced rank and had built up my own group of students and training location, or dojo, for quite some time. I had long had a karate dojo on the university campus, but now was moving it off campus. Most places in strip malls and standalone buildings around town were way out of our price range for rent. But the small rundown mall had affordable rent. Students had long done an assignment there that saw their observances and ideas sent to the management. When I suggested to the management that I would move my dojo there, they were amenable. We selected an out of the way office space type space with a huge common room, stand lone bathroom, and four offices. We used the large common room as the main training space and two of the offices as change rooms. Another room became the main office and the final room became storage. It had an external exit, so our early morning schedule did not interfere with mall hours. The floor was carpet over cement and the room was bare. We added mirrors to the main training area and hooks to the walls of the change rooms. We painted the mall entrance with a Shinto shrine image.

I negotiated with management to rent the space in exchange for my students' continued contributions and my assistance with vetting new renters. This worked well until the mall sold. A church bought the mall and wanted our space for their office. They were also not willing to entertain the existing arrangement. They moved us to a small office space above another store with no change rooms, no external access, no bathroom, and no office. This didn't last long. To get to the space was an ordeal. Marketing from that space was a significant challenge. New students had a difficult time finding it and we didn't spend nearly as much time in the mall. We lasted there less than a year before moving back to campus.

While observance of the space itself and a comparison of the two should be sufficient to make the point, the relationship to management changed. This should bring back thoughts from the first section where rules, expectations and culture often change and need to be explored. Promises, both stated and implied, must also be examined when we choose a location.

## Section Review and Work

1) Are you a creature of habit?

2) What new things might you do?

3) What have you always wanted to do but have never done?

4) Where and when in your life do you meet new people?

5) How can you increase the number of new people you meet?

6) What strategies can you use to strike up a conversation?

7) What elements of common places you go to do you tend to overlook?

8) What are the rules about observing people?

9) What are the promises made to you by the places you routinely visit?

# PART THREE

---

## Learning By Doing

# CHAPTER 7

# Tools

---

*Activity #7:*
This is a timed activity. Please use a stopwatch or alarm. You have 20 minutes to gather $2.67 in as many coins as possible.

## Money.

Some would say it's the root of all evil. Some would say it's a fiction. Still others would say it's simply a tool. I have to admit this is one of the activities that students enjoy the most. They see it as a sort of treasure hunt. I also have to state that it works best in countries that still circulate a penny or single cent. However, it can be equally useful in countries such as Canada where pennies are no longer in circulation, but many people still have jars of them. At the end of the 20 minutes when everyone has returned to the classroom with their change, many begin to see how the rules, expectations, family culture and even national identity have influenced their perception of money.

Applying the concepts from the first chapter, it is important to understand the rules of money. Historically, I have had one group create their own currency for the activity that involved a half penny. While creative, their classmate protested stating that it violated the rules of money; that it is illegal to manufacture your own currency. Still other groups expect there to be a mad rush to the nearest convenience store to acquire pennies and are often surprised when they are the first and only group to do so. Many expect their group to have a cup holder full of change or a coin purse of some sort. Students quickly realize that their own rules, expectations, and cultures have dictated their perceptions of money. Money is not to be shared. Money is dirty. Never discuss money. Never use physical currency. Always negotiate. Never negotiate. The value of money changes. The value of money is constant, but the economy changes. Money remains one of the most difficult areas to discuss and manage well because most people don't understand that they carry beliefs about money.

Typically, three methods of acquiring the $2.67 emerge. These reflect their understanding of rules, expectations, and culture as it relates to resources such as money.

1) *Win at all costs.* This group of students will find a bank machine, use their debit card to withdraw $20 (for which they are usually charged a service fee such as $3) then find a cashier such as at a gas station to buy rolls of pennies. Usually the cashier will force them to buy something in order to open the cash register to provide them with the rolls of pennies requested. But these students return triumphant to the classroom feeling quite confident that no one else will have the amount in ALL pennies. However, consider this; there is no prize for winning and these students will have spent, typically $5 to "win" the activity in which they were asked to find $2.67 in as many coins as possible. This win at all cost mentality reveals much about the rules, expectations, and family culture. When this activity has been done as a corporate activity, the number of employees willing to spend money to "win" increases. Here again, corporate culture, expectations, and rules may conflict. A company may be specifically looking to manage costs only to find employees working with a "win at all costs" mentality instead. Sacrificing personal assets to exceed expectations can lead to dangerous habits and an ever-shrinking box in life.

2) *Sole survivor.* This group of students typically has been waiting for just such a day and the zombie apocalypse. Somewhere in their living quarters is a jar filled with spare change that they've been collecting for years. They proudly retrieve this jar (the entire jar) and bring it to class where they nominate themselves as the sole change counter sifting through the treasure for pennies. The

remaining jar of change is poised on the desk with piles of meticulously counted pennies, compared to the penny roll purchasers that just have their rolls of pennies perched on the desk, typically $3 worth. But for the Sole Survivor, this has been an act of discipline, a learned behavior likely from family culture. A penny saved is a penny earned kind of family culture. Other groups may approach seeking to buy or exchange coins, but the Sole Survivor believes they have earned the right to deny other groups and to claim victory because they and only they were wise enough to collect coins. Having acquired, counted and displayed their $2.67, they sit for the remaining time proudly. No other member of the team needs to contribute as the Sole Survivor provides all the pennies needed. There is a pronounced sense of personal ownership and pride in the individual, but the group members often report that they didn't really feel like part of a group, but rather tag-alongs as the Sole Survivor retrieved and counted out the spoils. How does the Sole Survivor fare in a corporate setting? Often times we see the Sole Survivor with much coveted resources that they will not share because they had the forethought to hoard the resource. Think about the employee with a desk drawer full of post its or pens or packets from the local deli.

3) *The Collaborators and Rule Breakers*. Finally, there is a group that learned profoundly from the activity on rules and decides they are going to find, by any creative means, $2.67. They plunge into car cup holders, coin returns on pop and candy machines, and coin purses. They build the resource continuing to find pennies to swap out nickels and never quit until the time has expired. They ask class-mates for spare change and on rare enlightened occasions,

ask me. Sometimes, as the clock ticks down, they will find another group and suggest a merger. They will combine their resources in a larger group and satisfy the requirement of gathering $2.67 in as many coins as possible, sometimes even including foreign currency, calculating exchange, in order to include more than pennies. In the work world, Collaborators and Rule Breakers don't fit well into structures with a lot of rules but run instead on expectation and culture; the more creative, the better. I once conducted this activity in a government office and realized there was not one collaborator or rule breaker, but a group that simply gave up when they saw the other two groups.

Each of these groups learns something very different from this activity. Moreover, consider the relationship to money that creates these methods of funds acquisition. In order to do this, let's begin by examining relationships with inanimate objects.

Wait, don't think you have relationships with inanimate objects? How about we begin with favorite clothing? How do we care for that item? How often is it worn or used? How is it treated? How do we feel when we wear it? How do we feel when it is worn out or damaged? What about a wedding ring? A car? A car requires maintenance: oil changes, washing, gas, tires, and with each car there is established a different relationship. Some people even name their cars.

What about your house or where you live? It also requires cleaning and maintenance. The relationship is often different whether we rent or own the residence. The relationship is also different if we share the space with others and it may also be different depending on culture.

Family heirlooms handed down gain a connotative meaning, sentimentality, reserved only for that item. We carry the weight of that item and all it means. Everyone has been asked if your house was on fire what would you save? Families often hand down items as a rite of passage not realizing they are also handing down a burden.

Finally, what about your phone? Try giving up your phone for a week. NO? How about a day? I hear many protests at this suggestion. Many students have stated that they need it for emails, phone calls, coordinating their day, creating their schedule, or staying on track with workout or assignments. But the smart phone is new technology. It is possible to live without it, but then again, it's the relationship that's in question.

The same is true for money. This is part of the reason poverty as well as wealth are hereditary. We are taught as children what the relationship to money is; we create that reality. There is a vast chasm between the lesson of a penny saved is a penny earned and you have to spend money to make money. The first step in identifying the financial box you live in is to determine your relationship to and with money.

## Westjet Swag

Many years ago, I taught in Aviation Management. The students were fascinated by a low-cost airline that rewarded employees with shares. At one point the cost of fuel skyrocketed which resulted in share dividends plummeting. The airline sent out a call to employees to figure out a way to save money. All kinds of ideas flowed into airline management. Many were implemented. But one in particular caught the attention of the students. The airline stopped buying branded pens. Don't' all businesses have branded pens? Isn't this just a small marketing expense? The students thought this a pointless cut, until we did the math and examined behaviors. Most companies realize product loss twice a year; September and January. Why? Some employees use their workplace to acquire school supplies. Consider how many times you've taken a pen or pad of paper home? How many are given out at conferences or as a promotional item? How many times have you flown and needed a pen only to be given one by an employee; a branded pen in the hopes that THIS will somehow secure your customer loyalty. The company quickly saw the value in discontinuing this practice. At the end of each shift employees were encouraged to deposit any branded items such as pens in a box as they left. Those items would then be redistributed. It worked. Not only did it work, but employees started to bring in pens from other businesses and the company began extensive research into this form of corporate waste.

## Tootsie Roll, Pennies Matter

Years ago, I used to hand out Tootsie Rolls in class and then tell the story of this brilliant candy. Tootsie Roll was created during war time when chocolate was rare and similarly did not transport well. Chocolate melted. Leo Hirschfield invented the Tootsie Roll in 1896; a candy that lasted longer than chocolate and transported well. At the time, Hirschfield sold his candy in his shop. The candy culture at the time sold candy by weight. Customers would request a weight amount which would be weighed and placed in a paper bag. Candy was kept behind the counter and had no individual wrapping. The Tootsie Roll thrived beating out many competitors. But as the depression took its toll, many candy companies failed. The first thing to go in tight financial times are luxuries such as candy. Hirschfield pitched an idea to radically change the way his candy was sold. It would require a substantial investment in the company and a change to the entire business. Hirschfield suggested that the Tootsie Roll be individually wrapped, displayed in grocery stores in front of the counter and cost a mere penny for five pieces of candy.

This meant that an entire family could enjoy candy for a single cent and they could be shared as they were individually wrapped. Hirschfield revolutionized the candy industry doing away with weighing candy and placing a value on individual candy pieces. Hirschfield patents his individual candy making process and creates the concept of penny candy leveraging the pocket change of children; a previously untapped customer market. For Hirschfield, pennies mattered and built his business.

## To figure out personal concepts of resources, let's start with a few questions.

1)  If your bank account was a friend, when was the last time you checked in on them? How are they? Are they over-eating? Are they wasting away? Are good people caring for them?

2)  It's payday, how do you feel? Fantastic and ready to party? Anxious? Perhaps you forgot it was payday?

3)  This one is a little more complicated. As a child I would visit my grandmother. We'd play outside all day then rush in for snacks. We'd open the fridge and there'd be nothing to eat. Oh, there'd be milk and raw chicken, butter, and eggs. But no grab and go food. So she would direct us out back to the garden and tell us to eat our fill of whatever we found. I loved this feasting on blackberries, strawberries,

peas, and pears. We'd come in for dinner and there would be a fantastic feast of fried chicken, biscuits, gravy, mashed potatoes, corn, and salad. I couldn't help but think "where'd all this food come from?" But there were other resources in that fridge that I just didn't realize. What's in your fridge?

4) It's 10 p.m. and you've discovered there's a birthday tomorrow. What do you do to create a meaningful contribution?

5) A friend is getting married, but they don't need anything. They don't need money or anything for their home. What can you give them?

These questions allow you a glimpse in to how you view and relate to resources. Too many people devalue resources such as their own time and skills. Children forsake the highly valued homemade gift for a store-bought gift later in life believing the store-bought gift to be of more value. A member of my family always buys store bought cookies because in her youth, those were a luxury and only poor people made their own. Millions of people donate their clothes and items to second-hand stores or have garage sales. Everyone believes their cast-aways are of value to someone. They place arbitrary price tags on materials and often, people do come by and purchase something, but rarely at the price written on the price tag. In the end, a lot of materials are donated or thrown away. My grandmother, however, saved clothing, cut into usable fabric pieces and made quilts. She then gave away the quilts to needy families or sold them having spent no money on the materials for their creation.

Large and small corporations hire consultants to provide the same value their own employees could, but instead believe that only by paying the price can valuable information be gained.

Many individuals delay launching their start up, waiting for an investor, when much of the work could be done without an investor and through social capital. Some unemployed spend their time waiting for that call or sending out yet more applications to make money so that when they retire, they can become authors or artists.

But what about that birthday or another holiday? Many families have moved away from gifts to experiences together. Rather than spend money on a material item that takes up space or may be made from harmful environmentally unfriendly base products to sharing experiences. Consider what might actually grow the relationship or the recipient and give from that perspective. With this in mind, many have decided to take vacations, volunteer together, or take courses.

All too often people use the purchasing process as therapy; retail therapy. Believing that this clothing item or this beauty product will change their lives or that this video or this exercise equipment will finally make the change in them they desire. Regardless of how much is owned many come to believe that owning something else will create happiness. It does indeed produce an endorphin rush and a dopamine hit, but it doesn't last which means more shopping.

What investments, income, and resources are being swept away because of an unhealthy perception of money? We often ignore savings because we believe we can't afford it. We pay everyone else first, believing they are the priority, but don't pay ourselves for our priorities. We believe everyone must have debt today. We believe the only way to buy anything we need is through debt. We hand off investments to a professional; paying fees for their judgement. We discourage children from investing believing they lack the judgement needed to make sound investment decisions.

What if we instead assisted our family by purchasing, tracking, and learning from penny trades? We expect governments and corporations to have detailed budgets and purchase justifications, however, it's another story in our personal financial lives. We reserve discussions about budgets as private rather than sharing what we've learned. Perhaps we dismiss the suggestions we hear as unattainable or we perceive the suggestion as implying we lack financial knowledge. We expect our employers to invest in professional development and growing the company, but we rarely expect that of ourselves. We purchase gym memberships we use half the time and throw away half our food then donate half our clothes so we can go out and buy more. If a company functioned this way, they'd be out of business very quickly. If we treated a friend this way, we'd be alone very quickly. And yet, this is how we treat our finances and belongings.

# Pick Up Game

*Activity #8:*

This activity will take some time but involves your usual routine. During the next seven days, pick up any change (currency) you find laying around on the ground or elsewhere. At the end of that time, how much did you find? Where is the best place to find currency?

# Find a penny pick it up and all day long you'll have good luck

I often ask students if they bend down to pick up pennies. Nearly none do. I then ask about nickels, dimes, and such. One student conducting this activity found $23 in seven days. There is a perception that money on the ground is less valuable. Money on the ground is dirty. If I pick up that money on the ground people will think I'm desperate. If I pick up that money on the ground it will make me look cheap. If I use that penny in the cup at the cash register, someone will think I need it or worse, they'll think I don't and am robbing someone less fortunate. Ever consider that your tax dollars pay for the production of that currency? Ever consider how much a quarter means to a kid?

There are so many attitudes toward money that just aren't accurate or helpful. Rules, expectations, and culture also play a role in perceptions of money. Many families construct culture and expectations around money like it's impolite to discuss finances, or only poor people discuss money, or the man of the house determines how money is spent, or children are naturally financially irresponsible. Many people no longer balance their checking accounts. Online banking allows for instant bank balance access. We trust that our financial institutions look after our money and finances. However, it debilitates good planning and proper financial analysis. All good financial management begins with tough questions.

High schools used to teach basic financial literacy teaching students to examine their accounts and consider what expenditures were necessary and where were they wasting money. Bank fees are a huge contributor to waste. We often, for convenience, use banking machines which charge fees. Simultaneously, the financial institution may also charge a convenience fee for not finding their particular machine. Most banks charge monthly fees for accounts, particularly if the account drops below a certain threshold. The financial institutions rarely market that they offer fee free accounts for minors or students or individuals who fall below a certain income threshold. These institutions all fail to market that they offer counseling to all customers to manage their finances better; some even offer classes. People rarely shop around for a financial institution the way they would a gym or restaurant. They don't ask questions, they don't examine reviews, they don't visit the locations or examine the "menu." This is a cultural expectation that only fills the pockets of bank shareholders. There are TV shows, blogs, podcasts and newsletters that teach people how to better manage their finances.

We have been seduced by automatic debit, paying our bills without thorough consideration of the invoice, content that the bill is paid without fuss. Businesses know that laziness is profitable. Gym memberships, subscriptions, mobile device fees, all automatically vanish from our accounts and we rarely take the time to examine exactly what it is we are paying for. This passive consumption often requires more funds than paying the bill manually. Somehow, we persuade ourselves that it is money well spent, or we ignore the expenditure as common practice.

Similarly, we often dismiss existing skill sets. Consider that birthday, what if your skill is baking? Perhaps baking a cake would be appreciated. Consider my grandmother making quilts with scraps. Take a moment and make a list of your skills. Why? Because they represent opportunities few people realize.

# In my life:

Six times in my life I created ventures based on existing skills. Each time I found a way to create a venture with no money and using nonmonetary personal assets. At 15, I started a cleaning business. I borrowed cleaning supplies from my mother leaving her an IOU. I replaced those borrowed supplies within two weeks. I spent no money to acquire seven clients within the first two weeks.

When I finished my bachelor's degree in 1991, the cusp of the digital age, I taught area businesses to use computers to better manage their information such as inventory, wages, expenditures, and even customer questions. I started with the liquor store I worked for. Again, word spread, and I soon had several clients. Computers were not my major, but it had been a requirement for my degree. Rather than consider it useless knowledge, I put it to the test.

When my first child started school, I noticed a lot of kids on the playground and walking to and from school in our very harsh climate with winter coats that didn't zip up. When I asked a few children, they responded that they couldn't afford a new coat. I stated that it was an easy, cheap, and quick fix. They responded that their parents didn't sew. I began mending coats for $5 as zippers are cheap and the process takes only a few minutes. This turned into yet another venture.

A few years later, the school my children attended wanted to cut arts, particularly music, due to budget cuts. Being a teacher and musician myself, I put together easy curriculum for elementary aged children with some online content. Teachers needed only to photocopy and distribute the handouts, allow children computer access to certain websites, then 11 friends who were also musicians and I created interactive concerts covering 12 instruments, seven different types of music and basic music theory. This practice of leveraging existing knowledge to create needed ventures has unemployment proofed me and my family.

None of these skills are unique or particularly spectacular. However, with the right approach and the right timing, each was quite profitable.

There is a dangerous myth that entrepreneurs need a lot of money to start a venture. Truthfully, entrepreneurs do not necessarily need money to launch a business. But we do need to consider resources creatively. Skills sets, social connections, work ethic, underutilized space are all assets to be leveraged by a resourceful entrepreneur.

Social capital is vital. In other words what people do you know that could aid you? When I began cleaning houses at 15, I borrowed cleaning supplies from home. I even wrote an IOU to my mother and within two weeks, I was able to replace what I had used and purchase my own supplies. I started with the people on my street, door to door. I was known in the neighborhood as a trustworthy hardworking kid. I used that reputation and my mother's cleaning supplies to launch. This is both creative resource management and leveraging social capital.

The final necessary asset is sweat equity. That means how much time and effort are you willing to put in to see the venture succeed? There is a finite amount of time in each day. Some sacrifices may need to be made such as decreasing television viewing, managing time better, creating a schedule with dedicated blocks of times for tasks and strategies for completion. Even as I write this, I set a goal of 1200 words per day to finish this book. It would be so simple to give in to unemployment and treat it as a vacation. Beware of distractions as well. While writing at home, I am frequently tempted to do other tasks such as clean the oven. However, a trip to visit family in California meant that while they were at work, I had no choice but to dedicate time to the task of writing. But I have little doubt that the time invested in this activity will pay off.

Students tell me again and again that they have no special skills. Then through the course of conversation I discover they have many interesting and useful skills, I've had musicians, carpenters, race car drivers, beekeepers, and dancers just to name a hand full. But somewhere in their lives they have dismissed them as negligible or unimportant. The skills you possess are sought by someone else. I have come to believe that some well-meaning family member or friend has told the student that their passion or skill is not worth much and that a real job is what is needed. So, students put aside their interests believing them to be useless or unprofitable.

# CHAPTER 8

# The Challenge

*Activity #8:*
The Stanford Challenge. A couple teams work best for this challenge and you'll need three hours. With $5 start a venture. You must exchange something of value for currency. You must obey all federal, state/provincial, local laws and institutional policies. All proceeds must be present at the end of the three hours and the team with the most revenue wins every other teams' money.

I didn't invent this activity. Obviously, Stanford University did. However, they no longer do this activity. Also, they give students two days. Students either love or hate this activity. Either way, the results are very telling. I also make students promise to not tell other students about the challenge, but they always do. Knowing about the challenge beforehand does not create an advantage. Quite the opposite, knowing the challenge is coming and trying to create a plan actually renders the worst results.

In the classroom, students arrive, and I ask them to form groups. They are relatively used to this practice at this point. I give each group an envelope. In the envelope are the rules, very simple, and $5 cash. I usually do this activity about 1/3 of the way into a term. The students know each other and trust the process. They know that they will be expected to be creative and to not over think the rules. Without fail, three results occur.

Before we get to how the groups perform and what they do, the process of how they begin is just as vital. Many groups believe that the time is the most valuable asset and therefore attempt to do something, anything, as quickly as possible. Consider that if you believe the most valuable thing you have is time, you will never be creative; just rushed.

Others cleave to the seed funds and spend a lot of time brainstorming what can be purchased for $5. Groups also look at what can be done in just three hours. Again, this is limited thinking. If we limit ourselves to just the funds at hand, we will never be truly creative, nor will we create value.

Typically, no one leaves the classroom until at least 20 minutes have passed. Then they all start to feel pressure to do something, anything, and to leave the room. Understand that I do not pressure them to leave. They know they need to return to the classroom before the end of class, which is usually three hours. Some start to whisper, believing that someone will steal their ideas. Many will even leave the room for another room for more privacy.

The groups that rushed out, anxious to do something or anything, usually value their time as the commodity of exchange. They will exchange their time and labor for money raking leaves, shoveling snow, taking out garbage and such. But consider that if your group has six people in it and work for three hours at manual labor, they can only make so much; it's finite. Charging a minimal amount, these groups typically come in at the end of the activity with around $100. The group has hustled to get the work done and is quite pleased with themselves.

Is time really the most valuable commodity?

The groups that sit in hushed conversations, focused on the seed funds, usually buy something like a pizza then sell the slices, using the funds to buy more pizza, or donuts, or coffee, or whatever they think they can sell. But with only $5 what can be done other than a low-cost product? They have limited themselves believing that the best they can do comes from purchasing wisely with their $5 rather than ignoring the seed funds and focusing on their abilities or creativity. Selling lollipops at 10 cents each, however, makes for a high-volume low-cost venture that means they need more time to turn any kind of a profit. They typically bring in about $30.

Is existing funds really the most prudent way to begin?

The group that found another location to brainstorm usually ends up discussing what they have other than the $5 and discovers that they each have skills or resources to contribute. I have had musicians make custom videos to be posted for an e-transfer of $25 each. I have had a group with a beekeeper in the group sell honey out of his trunk at $10 a bottle. These groups do well by examining the low hanging fruit of current skill sets and opportunity. They learn very little and also make very little, typically around $300.

If we do what we've always done, we will get what we've always gotten.

Invariably, it's the group, that was the last to leave or that never left that astounds everyone. They spend their time strategizing and considering what the market needs or wants. They realize this activity is a unique opportunity to fail at no cost, so they abandon the perceptions of winning and instead play to learn, not win. They begin where this book begins, with the rules, expectations, and culture. They think about new experiences, strangers, conversations, and resources. They think about their social contacts and what they might desire. They think about their talents and how each of their individual talents can be leveraged. They struggle, they doubt, they brainstorm, they research. They create a plan and within just a few minutes make thousands. Yep, you read the right; thousands. One group used an online design tool and created t-shirts during a controversial time. Asking individuals to e-transfer funds or come by with cash they made $1,700 in just 45 minutes of sales using social media and a mock-up. Another group contacted their employers and created a unique subscription box business and within 30 minutes had made nearly $3000. That business still runs today making that group a tidy passive income.

It is the unique combination of what we bring to the table along with pushing boundaries that produces the best results.

Skills can only get you so far. After that you need the skills of others and to really examine what's going on in the environment in which you hope to work. The successful groups understand that time is not the commodity and that the seed funds are a trap. The real resource is the group and the cumulative brain power of those individuals combined with their social networks.

A by-product of this activity is that I tell students they can no longer complain about being broke. They now know how to make money fast. They now understand, from this activity, that their financial situation is a direct result of the perceived rules of existence and the script they tell themselves daily.

## Section Review and Work

1) There are many perspectives on money. Some are even hereditary as we learn behaviors surrounding finances from family. It is important to understand your particular perspective and determine if it is helpful and healthy.

2) There are resources other than money that are equally important.

3) What is your relationship to money? Like any relationship, how can you make it better?

4) What resources are you squandering through fees or devaluing?

5) What skills do you possess that could create value?

6) What people do you know that could aid you?

7) How do you manage your time and efforts to produce the best possible outcomes for your life?

# PART FOUR

Movement, Motivation, and Momentum

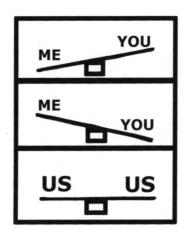

# CHAPTER 9

# The Feels

---

*Activity #9:*
You'll need a friend or companion for this activity.
Take some time and interview a companion to
determine their idea of the perfect peanut butter
and jelly sandwich. Focus on details and then
allow them to interview you. Be specific such as
who used to make your sandwiches when you
were a child. Are there specific brands that will
be required? Now, without coaching from that
companion, make them their perfect sandwich.

We don't realize the impact experiences from our youth have on our current tastes and preferences. Consider your taste preferences for this very simple snack. Who made you your first PB&J? This activity has much to teach us regarding our preferences, how they are formed, emotional attachments to things like food, and coping strategies.

Imagine you've just walked in a classroom. On a table there are six or so different types of bread and the same amount and variety of peanut butter and jelly. There are plastic knives and spoons and paper plates. Now, before you tell me you have a peanut allergy or hate peanut butter and jelly, or have a gluten allergy, play along with a sandwich-like-food you do like. We can get to the aversion side of things soon enough.

Even when given 30 minutes to explore the preparation of such a simple thing, there are details that get overlooked. Why? Because there are details that are so ingrained that we do not believe they need to be discussed. There are elements we consider to be rules, culture, or expectations that differ from person to person. For example, in your interviewing, did you first begin with "please wash your hands?" No? That's because we consider it a cultural universal. However, it's not.

What did you begin with? The type of peanut butter perhaps. But there are process elements here that are also often overlooked such as do you use the same knife for the peanut butter and then the jelly? What is the measured amount of each ingredient? Did you state grams or tablespoons? Do you cut the crusts off? Do you cut the sandwich in half? If so, which way?

There are typically three groups that emerge from this activity. First, there's the group that is thrilled with this activity and can't wait to make and enjoy the sandwich. They have positive memories of this snack and often still eat it. It has been described as "a hug for your stomach." They are reminded of simpler times and tastes. When students explore this, they realize this emotion is not because of the food, but because of the memories and feelings surrounding the event of the creation of the food.

This is how emotional branding is created. The same is true for cookies like chocolate chip or special dinners. The food is an outcome of the family dynamic. This group then begins to understand why they have a particular affection for certain products or places. Foods and smells are particularly powerful prompts for emotional branding. Some products just remind us of wonderful memories. Consider what is acceptable for a holiday dinner or a birthday?

There is usually a sudden "aha" moment also from this group when they begin to understand that other people have different experiences. Their experience is unique; not universal. Rules, expectations, family, and culture all play a significant role in the enjoyment of this simple meal. Many places in the world do not eat peanut butter. The financial situation of the family also plays a huge role. In corporate arenas, this group begins to understand why their product is not "for everyone in every market." They begin to explore the emotional side of the goods or services they offer. A student who worked for a car dealership began to talk about cars in a completely different way telling stories of road trips when he was young and focused on safety features rather than the color or look of the vehicle. He realized a 100% increase in his sales commissions in a single month.

The second group is the antithesis of this. They have a visceral emotional aversion to the activity and the food. But aversion is a powerful source of emotional branding as well. Students have disclosed that they dislike peanut butter because they had so much of it as a child. Peanut butter and jelly is welfare food or poor people food; making judgments about class and expectations. They might talk about how it's kiddy food, fit only for kindergarten. Or they might realize that their allergy to peanut butter has created an emotional aversion based in fear or negative memories. This is even further complicated by gluten allergies or insulin sensitivity or diabetes. When their partner loves the activity, it's an even better lesson as they become aware of varied tastes and ideas on something as simple as a sandwich. Reaching back to other activities, the students share information about alternatives and make a plan to share the food preference of the student experiencing aversion.

The students with strong aversions feel excluded from the activity. But in the journaling exercise that will follow this activity, those students are able to unpack the strong emotional reaction and understand how it has created limiting beliefs and behaviors, based in emotion. Aversion is as strong an emotional brand as family bonds or positive emotional brand ties. Think about the things we avoid like pain; many dental practices are successful due to marketing specifically to the aversion reaction to pain. Aversion can be created through past experience, fear, or avoidance. We wear our seatbelts, not because they are comfortable or that we have a positive emotional tie to them, but because we fear injury from accidents or serious financial repercussions from traffic violations. We avoid certain intersections because of the stress and fear involved in the chaos of that intersection.

However, consider where rules (laws), expectations, and culture collide. Texting and driving is illegal, yet many people still do it. Why? Because the rules do not yet align with expectations or culture. There has been insufficient aversion to texting and driving. The same can be said of driving under the influence. Some individuals have indeed experienced extreme situations and become adamant that no one should drive under the influence. Yet others embrace the culture of consumption rather than the culture of aversion or the rule of law.

The third group also has a positive emotional tie to the snack, but there is something missing. Some product or small step just can't be accommodated within the classroom space. Perhaps their sandwich requires toasting or they also like banana on their sandwich. This group responds in two ways: either they make what they can accepting that it just won't be the same or they opt out of the activity as the specific elements they require are not available. This too is very telling. It reveals those that satisfice and those that refuse to accept anything other than what they expect.

Satisficing, or accepting less but acceptable alternatives is a coping mechanism that creates emotional branding discord. We may find that childhood favorites just don't taste the same and likely never will, but we buy anyway in hopes that one day we will be surprised. We discover a long-lost recipe for our grandmother's cookies and make them, but they just don't taste the same. The other option is that we give up on the pursuit and the emotional branding tie is broken. We believe that things will never be the same. An author that no longer writes means that we will never again be captivated by the written word.

This very simple activity reveals the product and services to which we are emotionally bound. Research has demonstrated that we tend to buy the same products as our families; from cars to laundry soap. Those strong branding ties create loyalty beyond reason. This can create unrealistic expectations. Comfort food is only comforting for a short period of time, then we really have to deal with things. Still, weak branding ties once broken can create a search for product or service replacement leaving us always longing for what once was.

These are boxes of our own creation of expectation. This is also the source of issues such as emotional eating or shopping. The strong branding tie creates a brief positive experience. But because it is not a real emotional tie, not reciprocal, we must repeat the process. This kind of emotional bond also creates a lack of exploration or an unwillingness to try new things.

More importantly, this activity reveals the emotional box we have built around common everyday items like food. We create rituals around elements in our lives like this simple sandwich. We do this with coffee, chocolate, music, lunch, daily pleasures, bedtime, bathing, entertainment, and other habits. Couple this with concepts of money and we can begin to unpack layer upon layer of rules, expectations, and culture that may no longer serve us.

We select certain items in our day, thinking that it's a rationale decision, until we begin to examine the emotional connections. This activity can also reveal much about the box of time we construct. Many students assert that they can't eat the sandwich during class because it's not lunch or dinner time. What we eat for breakfast, lunch, and dinner can be dictated by perceptions of expectation and rules.

My family didn't realize the emotional salve of breakfast until we lived in China for a month. Breakfast there is very different and looks just like any other meal with wonton soup, chicken, and salad. The family found they craved the emotionally soothing breakfast foods of the West as we often eat breakfast together as a family. We still ate breakfast together, but I wasn't making family favorites. Instead we were exploring other foods together.

After a month, the family was happy to enjoy a family breakfast of eggs, pancakes, bacon, and such.

However, food can also reveal negative emotional impacts. After teaching Indigenous students for a year, I realized that when their families were placed on reservations, the government gave them food staples such as flour, sugar, salt, and lard. But these were not the foods they were accustomed to. Indeed, these foods created health issues that their families fight even today. Now, living in poverty with few resources and knowledge that was forbidden them gone, they struggle to figure out what eating healthy means. When you live in poverty you can either buy a small bag of apples or eight boxes of instant pasta and cheese powder product. One feeds your family for a day or two, the other can feed your family for a week.

We began the practice of making soup together every Monday. We used the school's slow cooker and brought in small amounts of ingredients we had. At lunch time, we fed dozens of hungry students and enjoyed each other's company.

## I hate tomato soup!

When I was very young, we traveled to another town to purchase a tractor. We left before dinner and arrived after dinner. My sisters and I were quite hungry. The person we were staying with urged us to ask the family we were visiting for food. The mother gladly made us tomato soup. We slurped down the tomato soup, but I felt quite unsettled about the entire experience. The fact that I was urged to ask for food from a stranger made me feel quite unsafe and to this day, I cannot eat tomato soup without thinking of that experience.

Before you eat your sandwich, share one half with the companion who aided you. Similarly, try their half of the sandwich. Take some time to chat about your memories of food and products growing up. Take some time to share understanding of the box that these emotional ties have created.

Reflection: Take some time to write about foods, products, or experiences with which you have a strong emotional bond. Consider what things are avoided also due to strong emotion aversion.

# CHAPTER 10

# Emotional Inventory

*Activity #10:*
Take a note pad and pen through your home. Write down the products in your cupboards or fridge about which you have memories. This works for clothes and other material products like furniture as well.

Our home is our mess; our literal box. The placement of furniture, the cleaning routines, the rules in the home, the expectations and environment or culture created all build a box. Do you have pets? Are the pets allowed on the furniture? Do people take off their shoes when they enter? Do people enter through the front or back door? Do people even knock? Are feet allowed on the furniture? Is everyone cared for or must they look after themselves? Is there entertainment or is conversation the entertainment? This mix of rules, expectations, and culture create a box, but how much of it is intentional?

What kind of ketchup is in your fridge? Is it there because that's the brand you like or because that's the brand that was on sale? Either way, it represents a choice and that choice illuminates the boundaries of a box. The bread we choose, the mustard, the cereal, the coffee, the meat or no meat. All represents a choice and those choices represent mental and emotional investment. If you don't agree, simply ask a foreign exchange student what they miss most. Friends and family are usually first and second, but third is usually a food item not available where they are; quite simply "comfort food."

There's nothing like sleeping in your own bed. While hotels attempt to provide us with comforts, there are often basic elements missing in this experience; our routine is impacted. Hotels use generic shampoos and soaps with different scents. Even the organization of our belongings can create a sense of security and home. The familiarity of furniture and its predictable placement also creates an emotional response. For this reason, most hotels use a similar room layout. We may not be at home, but at least we can predict what the room will look like.

When walking through a home, we may realize that a chair was a gift from family. We may dislike the chair and it may be uncomfortable, but we haul that chair from home to home, city to city, finding it a place of honor in our lives because of the family attachment, not because of a fondness for that chair.

A car may be a hand-me-down but it works. However, every time we drive that car, we feel the insecurity that comes with the life of student or that time in our life when we needed a hand-me-down or frustrated that we still need the hand-me-down or perhaps grateful for the functioning vehicle.

Perhaps while looking for something to wear you come across an outfit that no longer fits, love the brand and the style, but for whatever reason it no longer fits. Perhaps it reminds us of the last time we wore that outfit. However, there it is, still in the closet.

The items don't even have to be our own. I used to spend time with a friend thrift store shopping. Each time we'd see a wedding gown at a thrift store, she'd become quite sad and say, "it's so unfortunate." Confused I'd respond, "What is?" And she would comment on how someone had thrown out their wedding gown. This always confused me so one day I asked about her response. And she replied that why else would a wedding gown end up in a thrift store except that someone, divorced or dead, had no more use for it. REALLY confused now I replied; whoever wears their wedding gown twice? She had created stories and scenarios based on her own experiences to explain the dresses in the thrift stores. While I, furious about the disparity between men and women, pointed out that men rent their outfits while women have to buy.

Years ago, I was given an antique oriental rug. It's a lovely hand-woven wool rug. I hauled that rug through four different homes allowing it to dictate the type of furniture and the size of the home as it was quite large. Until one day I realized I didn't actually like the rug. It reminded me several times each day that my parents had divorced when I was young. That rug had sat beneath our dining room table when I was a child. I would hide under that table, on that rug, when things would get tense at home. I hated that rug. It meant that I avoided sitting in a room with that rug. We decided that rug needed to go into storage as it was creating rules in my life that were no longer helpful. The box that it was a family heirloom, an antique, valuable, overrode my own emotional ties to that rug. By addressing that and putting it in storage, I broke that box.

Students typically come to class and present their lists with some confused and some defensive looks on their faces. As students, many of them don't have the resources to choose décor but do what they can on a budget. Nonetheless, concert posters, pictures of friends, favorite items from home, strange second-hand furniture acquired on an adventure with a roommate top the list.

It's also quite humorous how often "construction cone" appears on the lists. These items acquired in a moment of rebelliousness represent the young adult breaking away from safe behavior, it's a physical demonstration of defiance, individuality and freedom even though 1 out of every 8 students has a construction cone in their room. Many more will confess they've dragged that construction cone through several apartments or rooms in their time at school. Even in higher education, the system is trying to create constraints of professionalism and expectation. That single construction cone is physical evidence that they can defy rules.

What about your office or workstation at work? What's in the drawers? What did you bring from home? What messages are placed in particular spots so you see them? Perhaps you have an image on your computer background of a vacation or a place you'd like to visit. I have had several offices and have learned a single very valuable lesson; never bring anything into a workspace that you can't take home in a single box. It's not that I expect to leave a job, but by investing personal time and property into a workspace I am mislaying my efforts on comfort not on work productivity. I am placing too much emphasis on the space rather than on the work. Having taught so many places I can say that space is often wasted. Universities love their board rooms as do corporations. But these rooms are largely wasted space used only occasionally. Money is spent on furniture and technology, electricity and amenities only to be used very rarely. The same can be said for classrooms. Even classrooms can only be used during school hours. Utilization studies have found that most classrooms are only used between 8 am and 5 pm. A few are used beyond that for continuing education. If we remove the constraints of space, suddenly, we can meet any number of places and creativity begins to flow. We as faculty rely on power point or technology. However, if we remove those old technology elements, we can be far more creative and engaging. We place books on a bookshelf thinking either that we will need them again or that they demonstrate how well read we are. Intellectual trophies are what they are rather than how that space might be better used.

Consider the customer experience. Many of the participants in corporate training sessions doing this activity do this at home, in the office, and where they deal with customers. The space where we deal with customers is often very interesting. Some participants have realized that the space was created for ease for the employee, not the customer. The systems and environment are holdovers from a bygone era that no longer suit the current situation or technology.

Every item comes with a story. I bought this desk with my dad when I started college. I found this chair in an alley. I pulled this poster off the wall because I went to this play and I know the actors in the poster. Every item comes with a story. The customer service desk has always functioned this way. The showroom floor or product display is based on an industrial model of consumption that is outdated and doesn't work with changing shopping habits.

The truth is that we value the story more than the item. Each item in your living space has a story. There's the story of how it came to be yours. There's a story of people who have engaged with that item. There are stories of reclamation or upcycling. In Geography, the story a place tells is called a Geospace. We curate our living space with photos and curios. We sometimes place things in a home to impress others, not that we enjoy. Oddly, sometimes our geospace doesn't even tell our story; it tells a story we hope others will see and be impressed by. It's common practice in the Midwest and North to have a front room with fantastic furniture that no one sits on and conspicuous vacuum marks on the rug. It's for show, not for life.

We register for wedding china that we never use waiting for that special occasion or out of fear that they'll get broken. But there it sits in a cupboard or cabinet still carrying the story of a lovely day and celebration of love. Antique stores are full of complete antique china sets because the children dealing with grandma's house after she has passed didn't want them. They had no memories attached to them. Mechanic waiting rooms are dirty and smelly accommodating the employee and providing only coffee and a tv for the customer in an uncomfortable environment. We weave through crammed aisles shopping among huge displays of identical product in varied sizes demonstrating mass purchasing and merchandising rather than the customer experience.

The customer has to wade through, sifting down racks of sizes to find their own, then try them on in a cramped stand up only fitting room.

What if your Grandmother had served that beloved PB&J on that china plate?

Is your geospace for you? Is it to impress? Is it stopping you from finding what you love? Do you love your office space and find inspiration to work when you arrive? Do your customers rave about the atmosphere?

As I began my life on my own, my mother gave me many pieces of furniture; a bed, a trunk, a small kitchen table, an old diner bench. All were antiques. As I grew older and married, my husband and I were given a dining room table, a buffet, an old chair, a coffee table, lamps, and many small knick knacks that had belonged to family. We acquired a few things as well but with so many antiques already it seemed that the only furniture we should buy, that would go with what we had inherited, would be more antiques or antique looking items. We had even been house hunting for a house in which our antiques would fit!

As our sons grew up, they came to hate the "museum rooms" and begged us to get rid of those items and update our décor. It took three moves and 20 years, but we finally updated SOME of the furniture. Our living room is now modern furniture, but the dining room still houses the antique dining room table and buffet that belonged to my husband's grandparents.

We hadn't realized how limiting the gifts had been until we shopped for things we actually liked. Suddenly we realized we had never actually looked for things we liked only things that would fit with what we had. We also sold many items, acknowledging our gratitude and putting aside emotion we sold or gave away several pieces.

There's also an inherited fear, a blood memory of hard times such as the depression. Our parents learned to hold on to things because they might come in handy. We inherited this perception and adopted it as financially responsible. We have jars of buttons and screws. We have 13 cans of partially used paint. We have half used roles of wrapping paper and boxes and boxes of bits of fabric. We have three hammers and more than a dozen screwdrivers. But a resource unutilized is not a resource; it's inventory and it costs money to maintain an inventory.

If the things you own are dictating how you live, their cost of maintenance is too high. The book and movie "Fight Club" states that the things we own end up owning us. (Oh, and we don't talk about fight club.) If none of the items you own appear in your dream life, then perhaps it's time to start getting rid of the unnecessary items. Fear drives hoarding. We hold on to things because we fear we might need them and that if you don't have them it will cost you money. Consider the relationship to money again. Well, having them also costs money. It costs in storage and mental wear and tear and carting them from one place to another. Consider also, when you die, will anyone want these items? The older generations are now downsizing before death to help their families deal with a lifetime of accumulation. We shop for houses seeing them professionally staged with minimal interior elements then we drag all our own junk into that space and wonder why it feels so cluttered.

Companies do the same thing. When I was hired at the college my office was dominated by a huge desk. This office was now for three people, but it had been for one. We needed to get rid of the huge brand-new desk so we could fit in people. In the anteroom there was also a huge desk and boxes and boxes of papers. In my office when I moved in there were three monitors, two memory towers, a huge desk and boxes and boxes of binders and books. We were creating an agile program based on laptop use. These huge computers would be of no use. I asked that they be removed but my manager had no idea what to do with them. They all cost money so they couldn't just be thrown out. But what to do with all this stuff? After a year in that office, all that material was still there when I put my own belongings in a box never to return. The college valued the STUFF more than the people.

I ran my own karate dojo for a decade. In that time, I accumulated many things like a huge heavy bag and a stand, kicking pads, shinai (wooden swords), and a makiwara pad (a punching board pad). I have a huge library of karate books and two huge shoe racks. I had truckloads of grappling mats. What to do with all this stuff when I left as sensei and moved away? My dojo was moved on to the university campus and needed none of these things. So, I packed them up and moved them to our new home. After a year, I offered them to the dojo at which I now train. They gladly took them. But why did I wait a year? Why didn't I sell them? Why drag them to a new location and store them for a year? Businesses also become crippled by the things they own.

# CHAPTER 11

# Drama

---

*Activity #11:*
Imagine you are heading somewhere familiar for
dinner, like home to your parents. Can you write
out the conversation? Can you predict the details
of the visit? Write that conversation below.

Have you ever had a conversation that seemed as though you'd had that conversation before? Most people have.

"Hi, how are you?"

"Fine, how are you?"

"Fine, how's the family?"

"Fine, and yours?"

Humans appreciate predictability. We ask the same questions and expect the same answers. We argue the same arguments, make the same points, and offer the same compliments day after day, visit after visit. But time and time again a student would express anxiety about visiting home because they'd once again have to defend their major, or their romantic interest, or their job. The student can often recite the conversation as it had happened in the past and how it was likely to happen again and again in the future. Frustrated, the student would often find an excuse to not visit home.

I hear from parents as well that they tell their family again and again to (insert request here) and nothing ever happens. Whether it be to walk the dog, do the dishes, empty the garbage, do their homework; they see the same results.

The expectation that by expressing displeasure or exerting pressure through conversation that action or change will occur is fruitless. Repetitive requests, demands, manipulations, and expectations often only result in relational rifts. As adults we perpetuate expectations and conversations of our own past. Either we make a conscious effort to change those conversations or we push them on to the next generation.

Students often report that they dislike going home because they'll have to again justify their major or their grades or their bank accounts. They grow frustrated seeking a way out and that often means either avoiding going home or avoiding the conversation by spending time with friends rather than family when they do go home, and the rift begins to widen.

Students report having the same conversation with roommates about cleanliness or noise or bills. Again, tired of the repetitive conversations, the students will begin to avoid the conversations rather than try to find a way out of that box. Many friendships have been destroyed by sharing living space without understanding how to construct new conversations or to express openly expectations at the outset.

But in all situations, avoidance only postpones the inevitable or damages the relationship. Another option exists.

The definition of insanity, as many have quoted, according to Einstein is doing the same thing and expecting different results. Once a script is established it takes hard work and mindfulness to shift the conversation. Consider the rules, expectations, and culture here. Consider the emotional investment in the status quo. Consider that the person to whom you are speaking has an expectation, their own PB&J, their own penny jar, their own perception of value. Shifting the conversation has to happen repeatedly for the script to change; once is not enough. The shift in conversation also requires a lot of thought and preparation. Desiring a conversation to change will not cause the conversation to change. It all seems like platitudes, but in fact it's true that the only thing we can change is ourselves. We can change the conversation.

How do we begin to change the conversation? How do we change the script? First, we have to understand the current conversation or script. Writing it down is the first step. Then treating the script like a movie script, go back and write in the motivations for each statement. What is the person feeling? What's their back story? What does their facial expression tell you? If you were the narrator for this movie, what would you be saying at this moment? Understand your view may be skewed. Try to see the conversation from their perspective and make notes.

After we understand the repeating conversation, we can begin to find opportunities to shift the script. We shift the script by being mindful of the moment when an opportunity presents itself to offer a different, off script conversation prompt. Statements are conversation enders, but conversation prompts provide an opportunity for further and different conversation. Many people are seeking the "mic drop" or conversation ender because they are tired of the conversation and see it as a battle or game. But seeing the script shift as an opportunity to take the movie in a completely different direction builds the relationship and creates new opportunities for understanding.

For years people would ask me what I did, I would respond that I teach at a university. They'd say, "what do you teach?" and I would be forced to respond with the list of very strange topics and courses that I teach. They would then look at me oddly, not quite sure what to say and the conversation would be over, and no relationship was built. As a communications scholar and practitioner, this was unacceptable. After a lot of thought and script analysis, I found my opportunity to change the conversation.

They say, "So what do you do?"

I say, "I teach at (insert institution here)."

They say "Oh yeah? What do you teach?"

I say "Students, sometimes administration, but mostly students."

They laugh and suddenly want to talk about their education experiences and a relationship begins.

My strategy is to try to incorporate humor. I'm happy to be the butt of a joke if it furthers a conversation or relationship. Consider a family member standing at an open fridge; a common sight. The parent, frustrated, asks the family member to get what they want to consume and close the fridge and the scripted conversation ensues. But what if we change that script with some humor. The family member stands in front of the open fridge door and the parent approaches and using humor from Monty Python and in their best bad British accent says instead, "Do you seeketh the Grail?" Or how about leaning in and listening intently to the inside of the fridge then saying, "You hear it too??!"

Consider a family member returning from school, tired and probably mentally and emotionally exhausted wants to remain silent. The parent wanting to bridge that chasm says, "How was school?" The family member says in a bored tone with eyes rolling "Fine" and the script continues. But what if the parent changes the question at the outset of the conversation? How about "How did your underwear hold up today?" Or "What off world species did you meet at school today?" There will be a moment of eye roll, the family member has been rehearsing this script all the way home. However, if the script changes each day, soon, it becomes a source of humor and release and a conversation starter, a relationship builder, and not a conversation ender or strategy for isolation.

These are relatively easy conversation or script shifts. More complex scripts require more work and more mindfulness. Steve Covey's <u>Seven Habits of Highly Effective People</u> includes a section on communication. He warns that we tend to stick with three strategies. We tend to attempt to show sympathy through a demonstration of experience, or we question, or we offer advice. Parents attempt to guide; that's their job. However, as children become adults, the new adults begin to resent the guidance and the conversation shuts down. The new adults want to explore their own rules, expectations, and culture while the parents want to see the value, they believe they embedded, continue.

We rarely invest in furthering the conversation. All three of these interpersonal mechanisms are conversation enders. Covey recommends instead, empathic listening. This seeks the script shift from being about mutual contribution to being about understanding the other person's perspective and experience; listening to learn. The listener first paraphrases what has been said and chooses to not contribute their own experience or questions, but instead asks "do I have that right?" Or "Is that what you meant?" Then the conversation moves to "Tell me more about (insert conversation topic here) so I might understand better." The problem, however, is that that too can become a predictable script.

Consulting with a large American company, they called me in as their corporate culture had become apathetic, unengaged, uncaring, and disconnected. I spent two weeks as an employee and quickly realized that there were accepted scripts in place. The company expectation of the appearance of productivity excluded spontaneous conversation. Employees became well versed in the passing conversation of hihowareyou,finehowareyou, but with no personal investment or care. Again, consider the rules, expectations, and culture. Consider the PB&J from management as opposed to employees or even customers. I started with a group of managers and told them to not speak to anyone unless they were willing to invest five minutes in conversation, meaningful conversation and they could not say "hi, how are you?"

The management team had to create, from scratch a new conversation starter that would ensure a five-minute conversation. Very quickly, the managers realized what they had previously included in expectation was ruining the company culture of inclusion and incorporated the five-minute conversation as expectation. I have challenged many to change this very simple approach to conversation. It is not an easy shift, but all have reported dramatic meaningful change to conversation.

Recently, I was called in to a meeting with my supervisor. He and I had recently had a very polite disagreement, but nonetheless, we had disagreed. I knew he was not pleased. He expected everyone to accept his opinions. As I came into the meeting the representative from Human Resources asked me how I was, seeing this conversation starter for what it was I replied, "I am excellent and am so glad you came all the way from the administration building for our meeting today." She was taken aback and didn't quite know how to respond. She had expected me to be sad or upset or perhaps even guilty. When I was none of those things it cast a completely different light on the meeting.

Changing the script requires a lot of thought, preparation, mindfulness, and creativity. Changing the script is changing the relationship. Changing the relationship changes the box.

## CHAPTER 12

# Rolling with the Punches

*Activity #12:*
As people present you with business cards, take some time to think about how the person made you feel. Perhaps make a note on the back of the card. If you don't have business cards for some people in your life, try to get them and make those notes on the back of the card.

If the person is a positive influence in your life, each time you have that experience with them put a small mark like a plus sign on the back of the card. If the person is not a positive influence in your life, make a different mark like a check mark. At the end of a week, check the balance. Were there more plusses than checks?

Consider again the first activity. What percentage of our exchanges with other people are a result of expectation? As we go through our day, we often overlook the impact other people have on our perspective, our productivity, our creativity, and even our mental state. So much has been written on office place toxicity that many have stopped paying attention and simply believe that this is how work is. Students understand all too well as they are tasked with group work. They know which of their classmates will contribute and which won't. They develop strategies to get through the class with a good grade rather than deal with the problematic group mate.

As an educator, I hear a lot that "the foreign" students don't contribute to the project. Having taught abroad I begin to ask some pointed questions such as: "did you as a group decide on expectations, deadlines, responsibilities and sources for help?" Students in China, for example, are tasked with making sure their classmates also understand the material. It is not merely the job of the teacher. If a single student in the class is not doing well, it is everyone's responsibility to aid that student. This flies in the face of the Western competitive educational culture. Remember the first activity? Rules, expectations, and culture also apply to education. More importantly, those rules, expectations, and culture vary from region to region. Remember the PB&J? Consider that you may be experiencing exactly what you enjoy while someone else may find a profound aversion. Where and when are you meeting? How do we talk about the activity or learning? Are we willing to try something we've never done before?

We start to contribute less and retreat from what might otherwise be interesting work. We are cheating ourselves out of meaningful educational activities and perhaps student exchanges. We simply do the work for others as it is easier than asking the more difficult group members to adhere to a standard, timeline, or level of productivity. We cling to the professional equivalent of old hand-me-down-furniture like power point or a non-creative presentation style akin to a book report. We think our most valuable asset is time or the small seed fund ideas offered as guidance from the educator, rather than pushing ourselves to the next level through creativity and exploration. We find ways to document our work to protect ourselves rather than attempt to more directly address the issue. We parent from a place of preserving rules, expectations, and culture, preserving the outmoded furniture once again, rather than pursuing what is truly valuable. Similarly, we discount the relationship and avoid conversation.

We may have other people in our lives that are a drain on our system and try so desperately to build a box for us. Some people are negative and constantly complain. Some may constantly question what we are doing or consistently express disappointment no matter the level of success. Still others may be our go to for energy and a quick positive perspective. We may communicate with them needing a quick pick me up or a creative solution. We may seek out people that we know will support our actions, no matter the action. We are seeking to confirm our own bias. We are seeking someone with the same rules, expectations, and culture, someone with an identical PB&J or the same hand-me-down furniture or we seek to justify that hand-me-down furniture relationship that no longer serves a new outlook.

It is important to take note of the impact people have on our daily lives, our productivity, our habits, and our demeanor. Only after we have noticed the impact can we create an appropriate strategy.

## Strategy 1) The Punch Card.

I was speaking at a high school not too long ago. I was discussing how my parents had always encouraged me and been supportive. I also mentioned that I limited my exposure to negative people. A student asked me how I limit the impact of negative people in my life. I told him that people have to earn a place in my life. If they are negative people, just like too much junk food, it can be harmful to my health. So, I created a punch card system.

Using the person's business card, I create a calendar on the back. I decide how often I see them and what is best for my health. Perhaps I limited a colleague to once a day. Once I have seen them and worked with them once that day, I put a small mark, or punch, on that day. If they ask to see me again, I simply say my day is booked with other things and I'm afraid it will have to wait until tomorrow. Now, at first some people will argue and state that it's urgent. But I reply that it should have been on the agenda when we met earlier and that my seeing them now will put off other projects. To balance my workload, the urgent matter simply must wait. They quickly figure out to have all their agenda items prepared. If once a day is too much, I plan accordingly. If they call and ask for a meeting, I respond that I am booked up until (insert date here) and would be happy to make an appointment with them on that day.

This can also work for family. Although it is easier if you don't live with them, the punch card system still works. In the lives of students, they might make chores, relaxation, and homework your priority. If someone wants to chat, you can say that you're making your schoolwork or other work a priority and you'd be happy to chat at (insert time here). I have had students living in a house with others actually put office hours like postings on their doors to keep would be socializers away. I have heard some say, "But I can't do that, it seems rude." What expense are you willing to pay to appear polite? Some parents will demand that their offspring perform certain chores immediately. This is obedience and highly valued by parents. However, as children become adults, they begin to build their own schedules and values. Again, the rules, expectations, and culture MUST change to accommodate the maturing adult. I have encouraged my own sons to consider scheduling time to contribute to the household maintenance and to make sure that time and expected workload is known. There are, of course, some variables such as sudden and unexpected snowfall or unanticipated guests. But regardless, the assigning of chores becomes a conversation of contribution.

Consequently, if the punch card simply will not work for the person, you may need to consider altering the script. In a recent conversation with a former colleague, they were lamenting on how they didn't respect their boss and how hostile the environment had become. First, I mentioned that I was unemployed. They were silent for a moment, then picked right up where they left off complaining about their work. Then I mentioned that as a professional, perhaps it was time to approach the conversation with responsibility and change the script. As a participant in the conversation, we also have some control. There is a time to be empathetic and a time to be emphatic.

## Strategy 2) The Dance Card.

All habits and strategies must be created with a balance. My husband and I started watching Victoria, the BBC series about the young queen. In an episode at a ball she carried a dance card at her wrist. My husband had never seen one. I explained that that's how people would arrange their dances rather than the current haphazard way. People would ask in advance for particular dances or at particular times in the event. He said, "Now I understand it when someone says their dance card is full."

The dance card approach means that we schedule the day, the week, the month, even the year. We make sure all essentials are taken care of and not rushed. Paying bills for example can be a great experience, if we change the script. When paying bills, I used to get very anxious and frustrated. But I changed the internal habit and script. I began to take time, have a cup of tea, review the bills and pay them being grateful for the services or products provided. In this way, I began to pay more attention to what I actually used and what I didn't. I began to pay attention to seasonal fluctuations. I took time to create a relationship with people and services and enjoy the time. For example, our family no longer subscribes to cable television. Why would we when there's so much online content and you can now route the online content through a larger television screen? We ditched cable for Netflix and Youtube. But now, monthly, I ask my family if they are watching anything on Netflix. It conveniently coincides with the billing date. We also no longer have a landline telephone. Why? Why would we when we each have mobile devices? We sit down monthly and examine the bills to look at usage.

Similarly, we must make sure self-care is included on our dance card. My husband schedules an afternoon walk each day. Taking that time to himself, he takes better care of himself; destressing, stretching, walking, and getting away from his computer for a period of time. We often rush through our mornings attempting to get as much sleep as possible while still making it to work or school on time. I once told my children, they could have unhealthy food and eat it on the go, or healthy food and take time to eat at home. They chose, after many rushed mornings and regrets for unhealthy choices, for slower, better planned, healthier mornings. As adults, both sons now do evening meal preparation so the next day includes well thought out and prepared healthy meals. This is also self-care. Consider at the end of the day to protect your sleep, have no screen time at least 90 minutes before bed as this ensures that our brains can proceed to a healthier slow down period and our nights will be more restful.

How many times have we all rushed through our morning making sure we are physically presentable; showered, well dressed, well groomed. But our minds are a mess. We spend more time on our physical appearance than we do on our mental state. This grooming of our minds, emotions, creativity, spirituality, whatever you want to call it, is essential to our wellbeing. Guarding our time of rest and spending a few moments to set a positive mind set before bed and then again in the morning can mean a substantial difference in the way we encounter and deal with events in our day.

Recently, a former student contacted me about meditation. I have meditated for years. Now, I don't sit on a cushion in a minimally lit room with weird music playing and chant. That is a common stereotype of meditation. Indeed, there are dozens of forms of meditation. He was struggling in his graduate program with focus. He lamented that he just didn't have time to meditate. I asked if he took time to drive to school: yes. I asked if he took time to eat his meals: yes. I asked if he picked up his phone out of habit when waiting: yes. Uh oh. Picking up a mobile device when waiting unless it has sent you an alert is a waste of time. We reach for our devices out of habit now to avoid what we perceive as downtime. But that moment of downtime can be used to our advantage.

When waiting you can use that time to meditate and clear the mind. We can even meditate while driving. Most people, when driving turn on the radio or music and sing as loud as they can. Or perhaps they turn on the news, the constant drone of repeated unnecessary information. Or perhaps they don't recall at all even how they arrived at work. But that drive time can be useful. In silence or with minimal background interference, focus on the traffic and begin to broaden your awareness to the peripheral areas as well. Make it a mindfulness game by keeping count of the green cars or the pedestrians. Walking meditation is also an excellent practice, marrying breathing and stepping and dismissing all other thoughts as they arise. Still I have had students also talk about the merits of knitting or other mindful practices. It is important to make time for self-care.

Also, on that dance card are appointments, projects, deadlines, meetings, goals, events, and the other goings on of life. However, we must also be careful about time aids in preparation, planning, and perspective. Technology is amazing at allowing scheduling. But technology, that lovely ping and easy access of distraction, can also rob us of our time. Establishing a routine may also be helpful. Your dance card should be as unique as you are. It should break boxes that may have developed and create more sustainable perspectives and processes.

What boxes? What time is breakfast? Is it on the run or sit down? Do you have a job where you shower before or after work? Ever consider an audio book while commuting? Ever consider setting an alarm to chart your schedule before you alter it? Chart how many times you check email, text messages, coworkers drop by, when is your most productive time or least productive time? Establishing a dance card means examining the dances on the schedule and determining which ones you might want to prepare for and which you might just want to be a wall flower for.

Finally, on your dance card, include people. There are just some people that make us feel amazing. Scheduling time with these individuals energizes our day and puts a smile on our face. Consider also, seeking out and including time with a mentor.

It's fairly typical for people to have a date night, a night that they spend with someone specific. However, there may be other people that you want to include on your dance card.

While visiting my sister and her family they often plead for me to visit more or to move back to California. I am a good dose of positivity for their dance card. BUT too much of a good thing can also be a bad thing. I tell them I'm rather like tequila. A shot now and again may be fun, but daily shots often creates a dependency or other issues. Similarly, the dose of positivity on a regular basis sees a higher tolerance for positivity and a higher dose is needed. Each positive interaction should feed your own ability to generate what is needed.

I spent the last year teaching in a program for Indigenous students. This program gave me unlimited access to elders. This was an amazing experience. I cleared my schedule to attend their teaching circles and made sure to incorporate at least two hours each week of individual time with them. The experience changed me forever. I received a spirit name. I learned dozens of phrases in Ojibwe. I began to understand how I give away my personal power. I also began to understand the value of slowing down and just listening to nature. I made sure to include elders on my dance card each week. However, I was careful to not take time away that the students needed.

In the realm of self-care, I also always include physical activity on my dance card; specifically, karate. I find karate energizes and empowers me in ways that other exercise never has. The teachings of karate-do also provide a path of peace and a calm mind in the face of turmoil.

# CHAPTER 13

# Checks and Balances

*Activity #13:*

Using an index card write a plus on one side and a minus or check on the other. Carry a new card each day for a week. With each interpersonal interaction, consider if you were a positive influence in the person's day or a negative influence. At the end of each day tally up each side of the card. At the end of the week, do the same. Upon reflection, are you on someone else's punch card list?

While examining the impact that others have on our day can be relatively easy, measuring our own impact can be quite difficult. We may have a very different view of an interaction. Carrying an index card may make us more mindful and create a system of accountability for each interaction. Similarly, you may ask at the end of an interaction if you can be more helpful or make a point of making a positive remark and always be sure to thank people for their time and interactions.

This needn't be a tiresome or self-abusive activity. Consider including a single word or comment into conversation. Some people will listen attentively making affirmative noises but no real words. Within your interactions, perhaps consider your responses. If you were to be more interactive what utterances might you change for real words? For example, someone tells you it's going to rain later today, you have a choice. You can jump on the bad weather bandwagon, utter an "ugh", or make a statement such as "Great! It smells so wonderful after it rains." If someone is telling you a story about an exchange, consider using words rather than only facial expressions.

"Well, I sent off my application to law school."

"Yay!"

"I don't know, I'm really nervous."

"Perhaps, but what an adventure and how brave!"

Consider this conversation over what might have been said.

"Well, I sent off my application to law school."

"uh huh."

I don't know, I'm really nervous."

"Oh, I'm sure it will be fine."

One is the beginning of a great conversation about possibility. The other is a conversation ender and an old useless script. One is positive and mindful, the other is routine, negative, and dismissive. This is the power of interaction reflection.

This approach is the beginning of accumulating the activities so far in this book. The rules, expectations, and culture of conversation play a huge role in responses. Many people have conversations focusing on when it's their turn to respond rather than creating a flowing meandering conversation. Some may seek to win at all costs by trumping conversation and one-upping companions in that conversation or producing a single innocuous statement to which others have no idea how to respond. We may be clinging to familiar conversations for comfort hoping to recreate a magical conversation of a time in the past; the emotional bond to the conversation still fresh in our minds.

A dear friend, and successful realtor, has an amazing talent; she asks the best questions and creates conversations in which everyone is included, valued, and validated. I once asked her how she does it. She said, she deeply values each and every person. There is something in every person that we can honor. She tries to focus all her energy and mental focus to the person in front of her at the moment. Conversely, if she doesn't have time, she is perfectly honest about not having time and states something like; "I really want to have this conversation with you, but I don't want it to be rushed, so can we visit (insert date and time here)?" There can be no questioning why she is an amazing realtor.

I'm reminded of a quotation from Abraham Lincoln who said of a fellow politician "I do not like that man. I must get to know him better." After reading this many years ago, I became enamored with the idea of getting to know people better. It's actually much more difficult than you might think. If you already know the person, they sense the shift in your interest and become unsettled. If you don't know the person your interest is an anomaly and again is unsettling. But once people begin to understand you just want to know them better it changes to respect.

For some time, I had a manipulative supervisor. I dreaded meetings and I often had to take a couple hours afterward to recover myself. In a new position I ran into my new supervisor in the hall and she said she'd like to schedule a meeting. She was paying very close attention to my reaction because she immediately put her hand in my shoulder and said, "Let's make it lunch, I'm buying. I get the feeling we need more time to get to know each other than a quick meeting will allow." Sensing my unease with "meetings" with my supervisor, she 1) examined the expectations both mine and hers then 2) considered the resources and investments and determined that 3) a change of script was necessary to 4) impact our professional relationship positively. She is now permanently on my dance card even though she is no longer my supervisor.

# CHAPTER 14

# When F*ck You is the Answer

*Activity #14*:

Take a moment, maybe a few and think of the times when you've been really angry. Think about the times when someone else broke the rules or violated expectations or treated someone badly. We are taught in polite society to walk away and not give fuel to it. We are told that Karma will take care of them that what comes around goes around. Take note of those times, write about them. What about society really pisses you off? Make a list.

I've been teaching entrepreneurship for about 20 years. It's one of those subject areas that sees a lot of debate over practices and approaches. All the studies that have been done about entrepreneurs have been conducted by academics that don't really understand entrepreneurs but bring their own filter of rules, expectations, and culture to their analysis. The big question is always; how do you find that great idea? A lot of entrepreneurship courses have students begin with a "bug list;" list what bugs you. But understand that starting from this place means you are starting from a place of fixing something and are already fighting a negative battle. But this is standard practice, so we include it in courses. I also teach a "love list;" or write down all the things that make life amazing and how can we get more of that in our lives. I also ask students for a "mash up." They make lists of trendy things or ideas and then attempt to mash them together with something else. Starting from a negative place often means that you first have to make someone angry about the status quo before you can demonstrate your solution. Sometimes, the solution is to abolish what makes you angry. Think about human trafficking, drugs, violence and try to think of solutions. Sometimes the anger and outrage about these issues overpowers all creative thought. Often the creative thought comes from finding ways to use things we love or mashing ideas together to create something new.

Similarly, consider all the people you know who would never let you change the script of a conversation. There is no way they want a predictable relationship to change; that involves way too much vulnerability. Some people will never let go of their negativity and believe that you limiting your time with them is selfish or arrogant or unfriendly. Some people will never understand the negative impact they have on others and you will likely end up having to be quite rude to save yourself.

I am half a century old. I am 50. I have been told all my life that nice girls don't swear. I've been told it's a sign of a lack of intelligence. Intelligent people know when to walk away and say nothing. I've been told to always consider the feelings of others, most often before I even consider my own. I was told that I carry the responsibility of how other people feel. I was told to kill them with kindness is the best approach to negative people.

Sound familiar? The problem with that is that we often continue to carry that with us. We carry around those hurts and wrongs like baggage. We dread having to spend time with abusive people. We spend way too much energy and time trying to find a way to deal with the situation. We carry them with us as a reminder to see it next time. We try to figure out how we contributed to the situation. But carrying around all those hurts and wrongs and violations only hurts the one carrying the burden. I guarantee the one that executed the wrongdoing is not missing a wink of sleep over it. But we do. We think in the face of outrage we should be inspired and have something brilliant to say. I also have to remind you that the wrong doers don't care what you have to say. They will likely not even remember it so don't waste mental space on that.

This is not an easy activity. But this is where we learn to process hurts. We don't do that well as a society in general. When I have done this activity with college students, they are often still processing things that happened to them in high school or in their childhood. When I have done this activity in a corporate setting it's amazing how personal relationships impact professional lives. People hold on to hurts for years and often find it limits their own growth as they avoid people or similar situations.

Three common responses come from this activity. There's a group that takes the high road and believes that someday the wrong doers will get their just desserts. There's the group the fights injustice actively joining causes and making posters. Then there's the group that just tells the wrong doer to fuck off and walks away.

*The high road* is indeed a difficult road. Injustice seems to be everywhere. We try to live better lives, produce less waste, be kind to others, put our money where our beliefs are. This can be quite tiring. There have been apps for devices created that gauge the integrity of a company. Is it fair trade? Is it eco-friendly? Sometimes the high road comes with crushing guilt when we find out something we have done has harmed others. The high road is proactive in most cases, but it also means we assume responsibility for a lot of actions that are not our own. It means we plan to fix things through our actions. Sometimes, that's just not an option.

*Karma* is a difficult concept at times. The waiting and not knowing if someone or some company is actually held accountable for their actions can be frustrating. What does karma actually look like? Does it mean the loss of financial security? Does it mean criminal indictment? Does it mean a scathing media story and loss of public face? It can seem that karma doesn't deliver the appropriate dose of justice leaving the believers in karma wanting more. Then there's the not knowing, the delayed gratification, if any. And what of those that continue to be wronged while we await justice? Karma rarely delivers closure.

*"F\*ck Off!"* can be a therapeutic thing to say. For some it feels like they are actually acting on their beliefs. It feels like setting boundaries. It feels like putting things to rights. But does it? Typically, wrong doers just laugh and go on doing what they do. They tell others "Can you believe what they said to me?" Suddenly, telling someone off or telling a company exactly what

you think of them seems hollow, especially when you realize that your Yelp review or letter to customer service or phone call to management means very little to them. It's a drop in a bucket of haters.

If you've read this far, you understand that we can't change others. There are rules and expectations by which we live, but that those are not universal. We can attempt switching the script for months and still see nothing change. We do need to understand that carrying around the injustice of others is not healthy. The problem is that we tend to do that. We carry around a list of all the rules they broke and how unfair it all was. We carry around our outrage and moral superiority. We carry our version of the story. We carry the preferred media channel's version of the story and defend our box. We say that's not the (insert religious belief system here) way of doing things. We defend our concept of rules, expectations, and culture. We defend our understanding of resources. We protect our personal social investments. We protect our politically correct phrasing and our sensitive positivity. We coax our negative energy back to positive energy. We knit for ourselves a new, eco-friendly, zero waste, culturally sensitive, proactive, straight jacket and neatly tuck in all our hurts and wrongs with us into correctly folded organized pockets.

Like many people, I could begin with a list dating back to childhood. But let's just go back in this century.

In 2012 I was propositioned by my boss. I walked away. It took me four years to report it. I should have gotten angry. I should have ended all contact and said, "Fuck you."

In 2015 a mentor of 3 decades told me to give up. I should have gotten angry, found another mentor, and said "Fuck you."

In 2016 a member of my PhD committee called me names and belittled me in front of the rest of my committee. I should have gotten angry, reported it, and said "Fuck you."

In 2018 I was fired because I reported my boss for an inappropriate relationship. I should have gotten angry and said, "Fuck you."

In 2019 my institution stole my research. I should have gotten angry and said, "Fuck you."

But in every instance, I was calm, professional, collected and simply walked away. But I was so angry and hurt and also guilty. I kept asking myself what I should have done. As I communicated this to my family and friends, I then shared that burden with them. They now had to carry this as well. What's worse is that in every instance, the person I was angry with knew I would just calmly and professionally walk away. They knew I would do nothing confrontational. Most, I believe, thought that I would be ashamed of the interactions. I believe they anticipated my response based on how many others had responded; calmly and professionally in the face of all kinds of bullying. The result is that I carry these to this day, but no more.

You must find a way to let go of all the things that don't go well and of all the people that have wronged you or wronged the world. You also have to let go of all the wrongdoing you have done yourself. If you don't, it will wake you up at night and eat away at you. But you probably don't want to yell profanity at people. How do you process these things? How do you digest something that has happened to you so that you can heal?

In 2019 I took part in a letting go ceremony with some of the faculty from the program in which I was teaching. An Elder had us write down what we needed to let go of on a piece of paper about the size of a matchbook. Then we folded it tightly, put it with tobacco in a tobacco tie and in a sacred fire, we burned them.

At a women's seminar in 2019, a session leader had us hoot and howl as loud as we could and as angrily as we could to let out the anger, the injustice, the fear, that whatever we felt. It was incredibly healing.

The dojo where I train has a punching dummy name Bob. Bob is the best sparring partner. He doesn't move quickly, he doesn't punch back, and he is silent. Bob is a great way to take out anger or fear or whatever.

Finally, creating new conversation skills means that I am writing scripts for situations like this that allows me to tell someone that their behavior is inappropriate, unwanted, and abusive. Early encounters with this new conversation method have made me feel better, but the bully or wrongdoer seems largely ambivalent.

## Section Review and Work

1) Over time conversations become scripted and the relationship stagnates.

2) Spend time writing the script and annotating the script with information such as motivation, mood, scene, history, and narration.

3) Create a single question or conversation prompt that changes the nature of the conversation and thereby the script.

4) Be mindful and creative.

5) Be persistent.

6) With whom do you need to begin a punch card strategy?

7) How do you begin to determine how you might limit the negative in your life?

8) What positive things might you include in your life?

9) How can you ensure you are balancing your punch card and your dance card?

10) How can you ensure you are a positive influence on those around you?

11) In what situations, in your past, should you have just said "fuck you?"

12) How can you better identify similar situations in the future?

# PART 5

---

**Where It All Comes Together**

# CHAPTER 15

# Pulling it all together

## Ogima

Leadership. There have been so many books and articles written on leadership that you could spend a lifetime reading them and still know nothing about leadership.

How many times have we each looked at someone and made the assumption that they were or weren't "leadership material." Based on what? What are the rules? What are the expectations? What is the culture?

Too often we assign traits to leadership that are unrealistic or just don't exist based on some past experience with someone who reminds us of that person or who had the same title.

We assume that the title and the salary must be reflective of something and we invest our time, energy, focus, creativity, and so many other things into individuals trying to mass produce positive results like a cookie cutter or assembly line.

Institutions create leadership academies and programs, online courses and conferences. But in the end what each and every one of these have failed to do is DEFINE leadership and realize that there are as many meanings as there are people on the planet.

I recently created a research project that was to provide much needed data to create a leadership program. I did the research and discovered that out of the more than 1 million articles and books about leadership less than a dozen included women and only two discussed Indigenous leadership. I understood in that moment that there was an assumption at work in the literature that all leadership was the same, varied, but the same.

As we reached out to interview individuals about leadership, it became quite clear that the connotative meaning of leadership to the Indigenous community was something very dark, manipulative, powerful, and came from government or corporations. No one wanted to be called a leader or to discuss leadership. We struggled for a month trying to book interviews. Then we realized this expectation of leadership in the language or rhetoric that was used. We examined it closely and changed the language we used. Utilizing the Ojibwe word Ogima (roughly translated as leader) we found individuals far more willing to chat with us.

1) We examined the rules, expectations, and cultures around leadership and found that the Indigenous communities had very different rules, expectations, and culture around Ogima. To understand others, we must first understand our own rules, expectations and culture and those of others.

2) We discussed at length the emotional elements of past research, leadership, government, positive and negative relationships so that we could construct a common understanding of Ogima. We needed to make and eat each other's PB&J. Emotions are strong motivations and must be considered. We changed the language we used, we changed the script and became more interested in the

relationship than in the project and everything began to work.

3) It is often assumed that when you visit an elder or Ogima that you bring tobacco in exchange for their time and conversation. Some people will hoard tobacco just for this purpose, already made up pouches of loose tobacco. Some people have come to my office, knowing that I visit with elders and asked me for a tobacco tie rather than make their own. Some people run out and buy a pack of cigarettes as their tobacco offering. We found that not everyone was interested in tobacco as the exchange; but would rather we got to know their needs and wants rather than do what was expected or the minimum that we could. Spending money on tobacco and getting the information at any cost did not prove fruitful. The real work of determining what everyone brings to the table and what the community or situation would embrace built lasting relationships.

4) After the interviews we spent hours transcribing the information and coding it into categories and themes that we might use to create an understanding. Some people listened to the interviews and thought immediately that they knew what the program would look like and they rushed off to create the course names. However, sitting at a table and discussing, brainstorming the gifts of each person we interviewed and determining the best way to communicate the content while also creating something unique took more time, but produced a much more rigorous program free of colonized approaches to leadership.

5) Not satisfied with just what we could learn about Ogima, we also looked at support services and determined

that every interaction needed to feed the success of the participants.

6) Finally, we included time and space for connections, for learning, for ceremony, and for iterative reflective practice.

## Shanghai

In 2010 the Chinese government announced a new initiative "2020". This initiative planned to see China go from a manufacturing economy to an innovation economy. Laws were changed. Education was researched. In 2016 I was asked to deliver a course to senior level students on innovation management. The government had already changed public education curriculum to match the new initiative. Universities were now also following suit with the blessing of the government.

But innovation management in the West is very different than innovation management in China. Many people point to the huge "knock off" market in China and ask; how can they possibly understand intellectual property? To teach this course, I applied this process.

1) The rules, expectations and culture of education and innovation in China are indeed very different. The definitions themselves had to be altered to consider differences in laws, corporate structures and cultural variations.

2) New definitions had to be built with comparatives and understanding the cultural and political divide between democracy and communism.

3) Working within the cultural confines of how universities work in China, the course had to be built to maximize

information utilization while minimizing the materials I would have to drag with me in my luggage or buy while there. It also had to be something students would actually use. Textbooks are expensive and rarely used after a course is over. Paper based course materials would be expensive and not particularly innovative. Considering the Chinese student propensity for sharing information I used technology to solve this. I loaded the entire course, power points, readings, quizzes, assignments, rubrics, and even the final exam on to flash drives. One flash drive for each student.

4) I persuaded my institution to give me "swag" and I bought chocolates that I knew could not be purchased abroad. I could have bought materials there but decided that the appeal of international tastes and branded materials, coupled with the unique classroom experience would produce an emotional link to the material and to the idea of studying abroad. I handed out swag and chocolates as prizes for verbal pop quizzes each day to encourage participation, individual articulation, and an abandonment of a fear of the wrong answer.

5) I spent time getting to know as many of the students as possible. I listened to their stories, concerns, questions, and conversation totally abandoning any thoughts of responding, but rather deep listening and exploration. I collected daily writing activities and responded on their papers at length. I encouraged them to build the files on their flash drive and even completing some of the final exam questions as they understood the answers, knowing that writing in English in a time sensitive final exam is often a recipe for failure.

6) I made sure that each and every exchange ended positively and always thanked the students for choosing my course and for attending. As any professor will tell you, delivering content about which you are passionate is very difficult to a half empty classroom.

7) Each class was similarly constructed and followed a formula but delivered on the implied promise to be Western, creative, and practical.

## Becoming Unruly

As I write this, I struggle with writing this. I still wonder how I will get this to market. I still wonder who will buy this book. I still agonize about every word. But this book is the culmination of these activities.

1) To write this book I had to examine what I perceived to be the rules of my profession. I had to look at my expectations and the culture of trust I established in each and every class. I had to break down the perceived separation of myself from classroom activities and demonstrate that I use these activities to this day to adjust my course.

2) Indeed, it sounds impressive that I've taught in four countries and at five institutions. But each of those experiences came at a cost. I had to examine my beliefs, my values, my perceptions, my emotional baggage. I had to embody empathy and compassion.

3) I had to examine what skills I possessed and what resources I could bring to bear to make this project work. I had to reach out to my social network. In the end, I had to take the leap and invest countless hours in the activity

of writing and rewriting, proofreading and editing and rewriting again. I had to consider what is it that I can offer? Is it my time? Is it my skills? Or is it something else, something entirely new?

4) I had to examine the conversations I was having not only with other people but in my own head and heart about this project. I had to examine internal and external scripts and alter conversations.

5) I had to look long and hard at my priorities. I had to dedicate time and mental effort that I could have spent doing something else. I had to figure out exactly how I wanted readers to encounter the information, use it, and what impact I wanted this project to have on other people as well as myself.

6) I finally had to tell the hater in my head to, you guessed it, f*ck off, while I write this. I had to do this not just once, but almost daily.

These are the living case studies of this book. The methods here have been proven over 28 years of teaching and are now being incorporated in higher education within some institutions. I use them every time I teach. I used them to write this book. I use them daily to challenge myself.

If you have to ask me if these activities work, I know you didn't do them, or you did some of them but not all of them. Maybe, you didn't want to incorporate others into the journey. That is often the case with self-development. We somehow believe that we have to do this all alone or that others will judge us for what we read or learn. Those are someone else's rules and expectations and they deserve a place on your punch card.

Reading this once and doing the activities once you might change a few relationships and boost your creativity. But revisiting this process at different points in time will mean that much of the content will become part of a practice of personal and professional growth.

These activities were created to help students, leaders, and teams see, explore, and understand the limiting beliefs and habits we all carry. In doing so, students gained clarity, leaders gained understanding, and teams gained a more functional understanding of the team members. Those who have experienced the activities use them repeatedly to understand blockages, politics, new venture stalls, and navigate pivots. I have presented these activities in classrooms, boardrooms, sales floors, and even hallways. The happy side effect of this process is that it makes change more easily navigable and can even create change. Understand there are those that will not appreciate the rules, expectations, or culture being examined. Honesty and examination can be quite difficult for some who would rather live with the fiction of the box they've created. No one can change someone else, but we can change ourselves and thereby change the relationship. We cannot, perhaps change an organization, but by understanding more clearly the nature of that organization and our role within it, we can better navigate it. However, most often, I have found that illumination through experience changes everything. It is my earnest hope that you have found something within this book that was illuminating and that you appreciated some portion of the experience. I hope that educators understand that creating meaningful experiential learning isn't difficult. It does mean that we need to relinquish a desire for the measured results WE require for assessment. Education is about change and growth; not assessment. If you're wondering how I did grade these activities, I graded the discussions, the written reflections, the level of understanding that resulted. I did this through examining the content, complexity, and comprehension of not only their own experience, but that of the other participants.

I wish you well. I wish you manageable change. I wish for you all that you wish for yourself.

For questions and feedback, we have a Facebook page. Just search Becoming Unruly in Facebook. You can also email me at oneclevercrow@gmail.com.